麦格希 中英双语阅读文库

学人生品质故事集

第2辑

王华运●著

麦格希中英双语阅读文库编委会●编

全国百佳图书出版单位

吉林出版集团股份有限公司

图书在版编目（CIP）数据

学人生品质故事集. 第2辑 / 麦格希中英双语阅读文库编委会编；王华运著. -- 2版. -- 长春：吉林出版集团股份有限公司, 2018.3（2022.1重印）
（麦格希中英双语阅读文库）
ISBN 978-7-5581-4780-7

Ⅰ.①学… Ⅱ.①麦…②王… Ⅲ.①英语—汉语—对照读物②儿童故事—作品集—世界 Ⅳ.①H319.4：I

中国版本图书馆CIP数据核字(2018)第046435号

学人生品质故事集　第2辑

编：麦格希中英双语阅读文库编委会
插　　画：齐　航　李延霞
责任编辑：沈丽娟
封面设计：冯冯翼
开　　本：660mm×960mm　1/16
字　　数：214千字
印　　张：9.5
版　　次：2018年3月第2版
印　　次：2022年1月第2次印刷

出　　版：吉林出版集团股份有限公司
发　　行：吉林出版集团外语教育有限公司
地　　址：长春市福祉大路5788号龙腾国际大厦B座7层
电　　话：总编办：0431-81629929
　　　　　发行部：0431-81629927　0431-81629921(Fax)
印　　刷：北京一鑫印务有限责任公司

ISBN 978-7-5581-4780-7　定价：35.00元

前言 *PREFACE*

英国思想家培根说过：阅读使人深刻。阅读的真正目的是获取信息，开拓视野和陶冶情操。从语言学习的角度来说，学习语言若没有大量阅读就如隔靴搔痒，因为阅读中的语言是最丰富、最灵活、最具表现力、最符合生活情景的，同时读物中的情节、故事引人入胜，进而能充分调动读者的阅读兴趣，培养读者的文学修养，至此，语言的学习水到渠成。

"麦格希中英双语阅读文库"在世界范围内选材，涉及科普、社会文化、文学名著、传奇故事、成长励志等多个系列，充分满足英语学习者课外阅读之所需，在阅读中学习英语、提高能力。

◎难度适中

本套图书充分照顾读者的英语学习阶段和水平，从读者的阅读兴趣出发，以难易适中的英语语言为立足点，选材精心、编排合理。

◎精品荟萃

本套图书注重经典阅读与实用阅读并举。既包含国内外脍炙人口、耳熟能详的美文，又包含科普、人文、故事、励志类等多学科的精彩文章。

◎功能实用

本套图书充分体现了双语阅读的功能和优势，充分考虑到读者课外阅读的方便，超出核心词表的词汇均出现在使其意义明显的语境之中，并标注释义。

鉴于编者水平有限，凡不周之处，谬误之处，皆欢迎批评教正。

我们真心地希望本套图书承载的文化知识和英语阅读的策略对提高读者的英语著作欣赏水平和英语运用能力有所裨益。

丛书编委会

Contents

The Big Match

Once, a group of boys decided to play a *proper* soccer game. Each one of them would bring something used in professional matches. So one would bring the ball, another the whistle, another the *goalposts*, others the goalkeeper gloves, the corner flags, etc....

But before the game started, while they

大比赛

从前有一伙孩子决定要踢一场正式的足球比赛。他们每一个人都会带点职业比赛中用到的物品来。有人会拿来足球，有人会拿来哨子，有人会拿来球门柱，有人会拿来守门员手套，有人会拿来角旗等等……

但是比赛开始前在他们挑人组队时，发生了一点小争论。他们决定，

---

proper *adj.* 真正的；名副其实的   goalpost *n.* 球门柱

were picking the teams, there was a slight argument. They decided that the boy who had brought the most important object would get to pick the teams. Well, now they couldn't decide which had been the most important object, so they thought it would be best to just start playing, using all the objects, and gradually get rid of what people had brought, to see which things were truly *indispensable* .

The first thing they got rid of was the whistle, because the referee could just shout instead. Then they *tossed* the goalkeeper gloves; they managed to save the ball just as well without them. Neither did they really notice when they stopped using the corner flags, nor when they replaced the goalposts with a couple of *bins* . And so they continued, until finally they replaced the football with an old tin, and managed to keep playing...

带来最重要物品的男孩将拥有挑人组队的权利。可是由于他们没法决定哪件物品才是最重要的，所以他们认为，最好的方法就是用上所有的物品开始踢比赛，再逐渐扔掉带过来的东西，用这个方法来决定哪些东西才是真正不可缺少的。

他们最先扔掉的是哨子，因为裁判可以直接用嘴喊来代替。接下来他们扔掉了守门员手套，没有手套他们一样能扑住球。不用角旗的时候，他们没有注意到什么；用几个垃圾桶取代球门柱的时候，他们也没有注意到什么。他们就这样继续踢着，直到最后连足球都不要了，改成踢一个破旧的罐头盒，他们还是继续踢着……

---

indispensable *adj.* 不可缺少的　　　　　　　　　　　　　　　　　toss *v.* 扔
bin *n.* 垃圾桶

While they were playing with the tin, a man and his son passed by. Seeing the boys playing like that, the man said to his son: "Look, son. Learn from those kids over there. Without even a ball they're managing to play football, even though they're never going to be able to improve playing that way."

The boys heard him say this, and realised that because of their *excessive* pride and *egotism*, what could have been a great match had turned into a shameful display, which they were hardly enjoying at all. That moment, they decided to put their selfish opinions to one side, and they agreed to start playing the match again, from the start, and with all the proper equipment.

And it really was a great game. No one thought about who was playing better or worse. Rather, they just concentrated on having fun and improving their game.

　　当他们在踢罐头盒时，一个男人和他的儿子在旁边路过。看到这些男孩在这样踢球，男人对儿子说："看，儿子。学学那些男孩子们。就算没有球，他们都设法踢足球，虽然他们那样踢永远不可能有进步。"

　　男孩们听到了他的话，意识到了由于他们过分的傲慢和自私，一场本应该很棒的比赛变成了一次丢人的表演，而他们也没有从中得到一点乐趣。那一刻，他们决定把自己的自私想法扔到一边，一致同意重新开始比赛——从头开始，并且用上所有真正的装备。

　　那真的是一场很棒的比赛。没有人在想谁踢得更好或者更坏。相反，他们只是专注于寻找乐趣和提升比赛质量。

---

excessive *adj.* 过分的；过度的　　　　　　　　　　egotism *n.* 自私自利

2

Balloon Acrobatics

The day finally arrived. It was time for the great acrobatic balloon competition. Every insect in the garden had been training hard, and now they were preparing to begin their *routines*. The balloon competitions were always something really special, since they could only happen after the children of the house had had some big

气球杂技

这一天终于来了。壮观的气球杂技大赛就在这一天举行。花园里的所有昆虫都经过了刻苦的训练，现在他们正准备开始他们的成套动作。气球比赛一直都是非常特别的，因为比赛只能在这个房子里的孩子们开完大型派对之后才能举行。要赶在孩子们的父母来收气球之前，

---

routine *n.* 一套动作

party. There was only a short window of opportunity too, before the parents came round to collect up the balloons.

Each time, the flying insects were *favourites* to win, because they could grab the balloon strings and fly off in all directions, creating all sorts of patterns in the air. However, on this occasion there were some rather unusual insects taking part: a group of ants. Of course, no one expected that they'd do anything special. They were so light that no ant had ever bothered to take part, but it was quite impressive to see all the ants all perfectly organised and prepared.

So the competition began, and the different insects took their turns, performing beautiful *manoeuvres* with the balloons. As always, the butterfly and the firefly left everyone amazed with their twist and turns, and their wonderful colours. When it was time for the ants to perform, it seemed like the competition had already been decided.

抓住很短暂的时机。

　　每一次，会飞的昆虫都最有希望获胜，因为他们可以抓住气球的线飞向四面八方，在空中摆出各种各样的图案。然而这一次，一些不一样的昆虫参加了进来：一群蚂蚁。当然，没有人期望他们会做出什么特别的事情。他们太轻了，从来没有任何一只蚂蚁过来参加比赛，可是看着所有蚂蚁完美地组织在一起做准备，还是相当壮观的。

　　大赛开始了，不同的昆虫轮番上阵，用气球做着漂亮娴熟的动作。和往常一样，蝴蝶和萤火虫用他们的扭动和翻转，还有他们漂亮的色彩，让所有人感到惊奇。轮到蚂蚁表演的时候，似乎比赛结果早已经出来了。

favourite *n.* 最有希望获胜的选手　　　　manoeuvre *n.* 谨慎而熟练的动作

For the first time in living memory, the ants shared just one balloon between them, and one by one they climbed up the balloon string, forming a thin black thread of ants. When all the string was covered, the last ant climbed over his teammates to reach the balloon. Once there, he climbed onto the top of the balloon.

This strange *spectacle* attracted everyone's curiosity, and they were just about to witness the most important moment: the ant opened his jaws as wide as he could... and then he stabbed the balloon with all his might!

Pssshhhhhhh!!!

The result was tremendous! The balloon began blowing out its air, flying madly about, here and there, doing a thousand *pirouette* , while

---

蚂蚁们有生以来第一次共用一个气球，他们一个接一个地爬上了气球线，组成了一条黑色的细细的蚂蚁线。当线全被蚂蚁覆盖后，最后的那只蚂蚁爬过他的队友够到了气球。一到那里，他便爬上了气球顶端。

奇怪的场面勾起了大家的好奇，他们就要目睹最重要的时刻了：蚂蚁把他的嘴张到最大……然后用尽全身力气去戳气球！

扑哧……！！！

结果太惊人了！气球开始向外撒气，四处乱飞，一会到这，一会到那，不停地旋转，与此同时，动作完全同步的蚂蚁在气球线上摆出各种各

---

spectacle n. 出人意料的情况   pirouette n. （芭蕾舞中的）单脚尖旋转

the perfectly synchronised ants, made all kinds of beautiful shapes out of the string.

Of course, that acrobatic flight ended with quite a hard landing, but it didn't matter. The *originality* and teamwork of the ant performance was so impressive that the crowd didn't even have to vote for there to be a winner.

From then on, in that garden, everyone understood how much could be achieved by working together. In the years to come, the balloon competitions were full of displays carried out by teams, and they put on some wonderful routines; something those individual insects could never have achieved on their own.

样美丽的形状。

当然，这场杂技飞行最后的着陆很惨，可是又有什么关系呢？蚂蚁表演的独创性和团队协作给大家留下了无比深刻的印象，大家伙甚至不用投票就知道他们赢了。

从那以后，在那个花园里，每个人都懂得了合作的力量。在未来的几年里，气球大赛满是团体表演，他们表演了一些极好的成套动作；而这些是每个昆虫靠自己永远无法做到的。

---

originality *n.* 独创性；创意

3

Fleabags

You know, they *reckon* Ken The Wizard and Clive The Magician had one of the best flea collections in world history. Those fleas were the cleverest, liveliest, strongest fleas of their era, and most useful for all sorts of spells. Ken and Clive never went anywhere without at least a thousand fleas on them, always

跳蚤罐

你知道吗，大家认为巫师肯和术士克莱夫收集的跳蚤是有史以来最棒的一些。那些跳蚤是他们那个时代最聪明、最活跃、最强壮的跳蚤，用来施各种咒语最好不过了。肯和克莱夫走到哪里都带着最少一千只跳蚤，总是安全地把它们放在他们稀奇古怪的玻璃罐里，这样一

---

reckon *v.* 认为

MCGRAW-HILL

kept safely in one of their *bizarre* glass bags, so that everyone could appreciate the fleas' special qualities.

One time, Ken and Clive happened upon each other in a forest. Chatting and joking, time passed by quickly and they realised that it was so late that they would have to camp out in the forest that night.

While they were sleeping, Clive The Magician sneezed with such magical violence that thousands of whitehot sparks shot out of his nose. Ken and Clive had left their precious fleas on some leaves for the night and, unfortunately, one of the sparks landed on a leaf and the whole lot set *alight*. As the fire started spreading, the two magicians continued sleeping, and their fleas began to look decidedly nervous.

They were all terribly clever and strong, so each one of the fleas thought of their own strategy to escape the fire. However, as they

---

来，所有人都可以看到他们有那么多特别的跳蚤。

一次，肯和克莱夫在森林里相互遇到了。他们聊着天，开着玩笑，时间过得很快，天已经很晚了，他们意识到必须要在森林里搭帐篷过夜了。

在他们睡觉的时候，术士克莱夫打喷嚏的威力太大了，他的鼻孔里喷出了千百个炽热的火星。那晚，肯和克莱夫把他们珍贵的跳蚤放到了叶子上，不幸的是，一颗火星落到了一片叶子上，把整块地方都点燃了。火势开始蔓延，而他们俩还在睡着，他们的跳蚤看上去显然开始恐慌不安了。

他们都非常聪明强壮，每只跳蚤都在各自想着逃生的办法。然而，他们还是在罐子里，每一个向不同方向跳着，这样，罐子还是待在原来的地

---

bizarre *adj.* 极其怪诞的   alight *adj.* 燃烧的

were still inside the bags, and they each jumped in all different directions, this meant that the bags stayed exactly where they were.

One of the fleas noticed how they were all leaping in different directions, with no coordination. He realised that they would never escape like that. He stopped jumping, and gathered a group of fleas who he convinced to jump all at once. As they couldn't agree where to jump to, the flea suggested that they all jump first forward and then backward.

The group started jumping together, and the rest of the fleas in the sack didn't take long to understand that jumping together would make it easier to escape the fire. So, soon all the fleas were jumping forwards, backwards, forwards, backwards...

The fleas in the other bag saw this and *imitated* it. The two glass

方。

　　一只跳蚤发现了他们都正在各顾各地跳着，丝毫没有配合。他意识到像那样他们永远都无法逃脱。他停下来，召集了一群跳蚤，说服他们一起跳。因为他们不知道往哪跳，所以这只跳蚤建议他们先一起往前跳，然后往后跳。

　　这群跳蚤开始一起跳起来，罐子里的其他跳蚤不一会儿就看明白了，一起跳可以更容易从火里逃出去。于是，很快所有的跳蚤都一起向前跳，向后跳，向前，向后……

　　另一个罐子里的跳蚤看到了这些，也模仿起来。现在这两个玻璃罐正

imitate *v.* 模仿

bags were now rolling backwards and forwards, towards each other, and with one last effort they collided and both bags shattered into a thousand pieces, setting the fleas free. By the time the fire had woken the magicians, it was already too late. Although they managed to put out the fire, their precious fleas had jumped far off into the night.

And nothing more was ever heard of those truly *exceptional* fleas, although some people say that to this day they still work together to help each other survive the dangers of the wild.

在向前后滚动着，越靠越近，最后碰到了一起，破裂成无数个碎片，跳蚤自由了。等到那两个人被火弄醒时，已经太晚了。尽管他们扑灭了火，可他们珍贵的跳蚤早就跳远了，消失在了黑夜中。

那些非常特别的跳蚤再也没有了音讯，可是有人说直到今天，他们仍然合作互助着，一起度过野外的重重危险。

exceptional *adj.* 特别的

Problems on the Ark

On Noah's Ark things were getting a bit boring. Noah and his animals had spent so many days *secluded* there that they started organising games and activities to amuse themselves. But, with all that *pent-up* energy, the games got rather *rowdy* , and a woodpecker ended up drilling a hole in the bottom of the ark. As water

方舟上的难题

在挪亚方舟上，日子变得有些无聊起来。诺亚和他的动物们与世隔绝在方舟上待了好多天了，他们开始组织游戏和活动自娱自乐。但是，他们压抑了很久的精力使游戏场面变得相当吵闹。啄木鸟最后竟在方舟底上啄出了个洞。随着水开始流进船里，洞变得越来越大。所

seclude *v.* 隔离
rowdy *adj.* 吵闹的

pent-up *adj.* 压抑的；积压的

began entering the boat, the hole got bigger. So, more water came in, and things got a bit worrying.

One by one, different animals tried to fix the hole. They even got competitive about it because everyone wanted to be the animal that had saved the ark. The *beaver* built a dam over the hole, but not even that worked. Everyone was scared, worried that the boat would sink. That was, until the bee started talking. The bee explained to everyone how it was that bees always worked together, as a team, each one doing the job they were best at. On hearing this, all the animals set about working together, each one playing their part by contributing their own special talent. The birds grabbed onto parts of the ark with their beaks, and flapped their wings furiously, lifting the boat up a little. The elephants sucked up the water in their *trunks* and shot it back into the sea. The fastest animals ran here and there,

---

以，更多的水流了进来，局面变得令人担忧起来。

各种动物一个接一个地试图把洞补好。他们甚至把这当成了比赛，因为谁都想做拯救方舟的那一个。海狸在洞的四周筑起一道堤坝都没起作用。大家都害怕了，担心着船会沉下去。过了一会儿，蜜蜂说话了。蜜蜂告诉大家他们是如何一起作为一个团队进行合作的，每一只蜜蜂做自己最擅长的部分。听到这，所有的动物都开始合作起来，每一个都发挥着他们特殊的才能。鸟儿们用他们的嘴衔着船上的部件，猛烈地扇动着翅膀，把船身抬起了一点。大象用他们的长鼻子吸着水，然后喷回大海里。跑得最快的动物们跑这跑那，收集着材料。那些习惯筑巢的动物接过这些材料很

---

beaver *n.* 海狸

trunk *n.* 象鼻

collecting materials. Those used to making nests took this material and stuffed it quickly into the hole.

And so, working together, the animals managed to reduce the amount of water coming into the ark, but they still hadn't stopped it completely. Desperate, they kept asking each other if there were any other animals that could help. They searched and searched, but there were no other animals left in the ark. Then, suddenly, a little fish swam in through the hole. The animals realised that they still had not asked for help from all the sea creatures. They asked the little fish to go and *summon* help to save their boat. He swam off and soon fish after fish arrived at the ark. Even a big whale came, and the whale pressed its great *belly* against the hole in the ship. This stopped any more water entering, and it gave the animals on the ark time to close up the hole.

快塞进洞里。

　　就这样，动物们一起合作，设法让进入方舟的水减少了，可是他们仍然没有完全阻止水流进来。他们绝望地不停互相问着，有没有其他动物可以帮忙。他们找啊找，可是方舟里没有别的动物了。然后，突然一条小鱼从洞里游了进来。动物们意识到他们还没有请海里的生物们帮忙呢。他们请求小鱼去召集其他帮手来帮忙拯救他们的船。小鱼游走了，很快一条接一条的鱼来到了方舟。甚至还来了一条大鲸鱼，鲸鱼用他的大肚子堵在了船洞上。这样，水再也进不来了，给方舟上的动物们足够的时间把洞给封上了。

---

summon　*v.* 召集；召唤　　　　　　　　　　belly　*n.* 腹部；肚子

5

The Tree and the Vegetables

Once upon a time, there was a lovely vegetable *patch*, on which grew a very *leafy* tree. Both the patch and the tree gave the place a wonderful appearance, and were the pride and joy of the garden's owner. What no one knew was that the vegetables in the patch and the tree couldn't stand each other. The vegetables

大树和蔬菜

从前，有一个可爱的菜园，里面长着一棵枝叶茂盛的大树。菜园和大树让那块地方看起来很美好，它们是花园主人的骄傲和快乐。没有人知道的是，菜园里的蔬菜和大树无法忍受彼此。蔬菜讨厌大树的影子，因为影子使得它们只能得到一点儿赖以生存的阳光。另一方面，

---

patch *n.* 小块土地；菜园   leafy *adj.* 叶茂盛的；多叶的

hated the tree's shadow, because it left them only just enough light to survive. The tree, on the other hand, *resented* the vegetables because they drank nearly all the water before it could get to him, leaving him with just enough to survive.

The situation became so extreme that the vegetables got totally fed up and decided to use up all the water in the ground so that the tree would dry up. The tree answered back by refusing to shade the vegetables from the hot midday sun, so they too began to dry up. Before long, the vegetables were really *scrawny*, and the tree's branches were drying up.

None of them suspected that the *gardener*, on seeing his vegetable patch *deteriorating*, would stop watering it. When he did that, both the tree and the vegetables really learned what thirst was. There seemed to be no solution, but one of the vegetables, a small courgette,

---

大树也憎恨蔬菜，因为水还没流到大树这里就基本被蔬菜喝光了，只留给它一点点仅供生存的水。

后来情况走向了极端，蔬菜彻底不耐烦了，于是决定用光地里所有的水，好让大树干枯。为了报复，大树不再给蔬菜遮阴，让它们在正午饱受太阳的暴晒，这样它们也开始干枯了。不久，蔬菜真的变得瘦骨伶仃，而大树的树枝也干枯了。

没有人想到园丁在看到他的菜园正在恶化之后会停止浇水。当他真的停止浇水时，大树和蔬菜都真正了解到了什么是口渴。好像没有解决的办法了，可是其中一个蔬菜小胡瓜明白出了什么问题，于是决定解决问题。

---

resent *v.* 愤恨；憎恶　　　　　　　scrawny *adj.* 干瘦的；骨瘦如柴的
gardener *n.* 园丁；花匠　　　　　　deteriorate *v.* 恶化；变坏

understood what was going on, and decided to resolve it. Despite the little water available, and the unforgiving heat, the little courgette did all he could to grow, grow, grow...

He managed to grow so big that the gardener started watering the patch again. Now the gardener wanted to enter that beautiful big courgette in some gardening contest.

And so it was that the vegetables and the tree realised that it was better to help each other than to fight. They should really learn how to live in *harmony* with those around them, doing the best they could. So they decided to work together, using both the shade and the water in the best combination to grow good vegetables. Seeing how well they were doing, the gardener now gave the best of care to his vegetable patch, watering and *fertilising* it better than any other patch for miles around.

尽管水很少，还要忍受酷热，小胡瓜尽了一切可能努力地生长、生长、生长……

小胡瓜终于长得特别大，园丁又开始给菜园浇水了。现在园丁想拿这棵漂亮的大胡瓜去参加园艺大赛。

就这样，蔬菜和大树意识到，互相帮助要好过彼此争斗。它们真应该学习如何尽量与周围的事物和谐地生活。所以它们决定合作，让树荫和水完美搭配，好长出优良的蔬菜。看到蔬菜长势这么好，园丁现在精心照顾他的菜园，给它们浇水、施肥，比方圆几英里的菜园照顾得都要好。

---

harmony *n.* 和睦，融洽

fertilise *v.* 施肥于；使肥沃

6

Billy Peck, Tightrope Waddler

Billy Peck was a farm duck whose big dream was to become a *tightrope* walker. Every day he spent hours out on the rope, practicing, encouraged by his *faithful* friend, Artie Quack. Artie was an older duck who, when young, had practiced that very same art. Both of them were a bit flap-footed at it, but they had

走钢丝的比利·派克

比利·派克是农场里的一只鸭子，他的梦想是做一名走钢丝的演员。他每天都要花好几个小时练习走钢丝，并且得到了他忠实的朋友阿迪·夸克的鼓励。阿迪是一只比比利年长的鸭子，他年轻的时候也练习过走钢丝。他们俩的双脚都有点儿扁平，但这丝毫没有阻碍他们继

tightrope *n.* （尤指马戏团表演用的）绷　　　　faithful *adj.* 忠实的；可靠的
　　　　　　紧的绳索或钢丝

never let that get in the way of doing all they could to keep training and hopefully improve.

One day, a new *ram* arrived at the farm. Soon after noticing the ducks' tightrope practice, he came over and began praising them. He said they were doing great, and he bet they could cross any *precipice* on that rope of theirs. This left Billy feeling highly encouraged, despite Artie commenting that he hadn't noticed any real improvement.

A few days later, Billy found himself with the ram, looking across a *ravine* . The gap was so wide that no one could jump it. You could only cross it using a tightrope. Artie tried to talk his friend out of it. He wanted him to realise that he wasn't such a great tightrope walker, and this thing with the ravine would be really dangerous. The ram disagreed, assuring them that Billy Peck was the best tightrope walker in the whole region, and that Artie Quack was just jealous

---

续训练，他们很希望能够取得进步。

一天，农场来了一只公羊。看到两只鸭子练习走钢丝之后，公羊马上走上前去称赞他们。他说他们走得非常好，并且相信他们能靠走钢丝跨过任何悬崖。这让比利倍受鼓舞，尽管阿迪说他并没有看到一点儿实质性的进步。

几天以后，比利和公羊同时站在山谷的一边望向另一边。间隔太宽了，谁也跳不过去，只有用钢丝才能跨过去。阿迪劝比利不要这么做，他想让比利意识到，他走钢丝的技巧其实不怎么好，而且利用走钢丝跨越山谷非常危险。可是公羊不同意，他向他们保证，说比利·派克是整个地区

---

ram *n.* 公羊   precipice *n.* 悬崖；绝壁
ravine *n.* 沟壑；溪谷

of him. Both ducks got angry, and Artie refused to help with the tightrope walk.

On the ravine, the ram *egged Billy on to reach* the other side. But as soon as he had stepped out onto the rope Billy lost his balance, and fell. Fortunately he landed on a small *ledge* , but when he asked the ram to help him up, he discovered that he had disappeared. Billy Peck had to spend quite some time there, and even worse, his leg was broken.

He realised that his old friend Artie had been telling him the truth all along. He saw that it couldn't have been easy for Artie to tell him that he wasn't a good tightrope walker, and Billy was grateful to have such a good friend who would always tell him the truth...

And Artie really was a good friend, because, knowing what was about to happen, he had gone straight off to find a group of wild

---

最棒的钢丝表演者，还说阿迪·夸克只是嫉妒比利而已。两只鸭子都很生气，阿迪拒绝帮助比利走钢丝。

在山谷边上，公羊怂恿比利走到山谷的另一边。可是刚刚走上钢丝，比利就失去平衡掉了下去。幸好他掉到了一块小岩石架上，可是当他让公羊帮他上去的时候，他发现公羊已经不见了。比利·派克不得不在下面待了很长时间，更糟糕的是，他的腿摔断了。

他意识到，他的老朋友阿迪一直都在跟他说真话。他看得出来，阿迪告诉他，他不是个出色的钢丝表演者，说出这句话对阿迪来说一定很不容易。拥有一个一直跟他说实话的好朋友，比利感到很庆幸……

阿迪真的是个非常好的朋友，因为他知道会发生什么事，所以马上去

---

egg sb. on to do sth.　怂恿或鼓励
　　　　　　　　　　　某人做某事

ledge *n.* 岩架；悬崖岩石突出部

ducks — old friends of his. These wild ducks flew much better than the poor old farm ducks. Artie prepared a rescue operation with the wild ducks.

Billy asked Artie to forgive him, and Artie happily did so. And, while being rescued, and flying high, Billy could see that over on the other side of the ravine there was a load of well-hidden and delicious *delicacies* . Billy realised that that was all the greedy ram had been interested in. He wanted those foods, but couldn't cross the ravine himself, so had tried to use Billy to get them.

Billy felt foolish, but also fortunate, because helped by his new duck friends they managed to gather all that wonderful food, take it to the farm, and have a big party among real friends.

找他的老朋友———一群野鸭子来帮忙。这群野鸭子比农场里那些可怜的老鸭子的飞行技术要高多了。阿迪和野鸭子们准备好了救援行动。

比利请求阿迪原谅他，而阿迪也高兴地原谅了比利。当比利得救并且飞得很高的时候，他看见山谷的另一边有很多隐藏得十分严密的可口美味。比利终于明白，原来那才是贪婪的公羊所感兴趣的东西。他想要那些食物，可是自己又过不去，所以才利用比利过去拿。

比利觉得自己很愚蠢却又很幸运，因为在新鸭子朋友的帮助下，他们得以获得全部的美食，并拿回农场，和真正的朋友们一起举办了一场盛大的聚会。

---

delicacy *n.* 珍馐；佳肴

The Crashed Martian

One night, a hedgehog was *scanning* the sky with his telescope, when he saw what seemed to be a spaceship flying to the moon. When he managed to properly focus on it, he found out that it was a craft belonging to an unfortunate *Martian* who seemed to have had an accident, and had to make an emergency landing on the moon.

坠落的火星人

天夜晚，一只刺猬正在用他的望远镜观测夜空，这时他看见好像有只宇宙飞船正朝月球飞去。当他把焦点集中在宇宙飞船上时，他发现那是一艘属于一个不幸的火星人的飞船，火星人好像发生了意外，不得不紧急降落在月球上。

scan v. 细看　　　　　　　　　　　　　Martian n. 火星人

The hedgehog realised that surely only he himself had seen this, so he decided to try to save the Martian. He called together a few animals to help. They couldn't think what to do, so they called for more and more animals to join in. In the end, practically everyone in the forest was involved. It occurred to them that if they stood on top of each other, they could build a big tower and perhaps reach the moon.

That proved somewhat difficult, and most animals ended up having had a finger in their eye, someone's foot in their ear, and numerous bumps on the head. However, after much perseverance, they finally reached the moon and rescued the Martian. Most unfortunately, while he was coming down the tower of animals, the bear couldn't help sneezing. He happened to be *allergic* to moon dust.

The whole tower crashed to Earth with a great *din comprising howls*

刺猬确信只有他自己看到了这一幕，所以他决定去救那个火星人。他召集了一些动物帮忙。这些动物不知道该怎么办，所以他们又叫了越来越多的动物来帮忙。结果，森林里所有的动物都来了。他们想到，如果他们一个踩着另一个的肩膀叠罗汉，就能搭成一座高塔，也许能够到达月球。

事实证明这很难。大多数动物的眼睛被别人的手指戳到了，或者是耳朵被别人的脚给踩到了，大家的头也不断被撞到。不过大家坚持住了，最后到了月球，救了火星人。最不幸的是，当火星人顺着动物们搭成的塔往下爬的时候，熊忍不住打了个喷嚏，他正巧对月球上的灰尘过敏。

整座塔倒在了地球上，引起了一阵喧闹，动物们有的长嚎，有的吼

---

allergic *adj.* 过敏的
comprise *v.* 包含；构成

din *n.* 嘈杂声；吵闹声
howl *n.* 长嚎；喊叫声

, roars , and other assorted animal cries. Seeing all this, the Martian thought that the animals would be very angry with him because they would blame it all on him.

But it was just the opposite. As they recovered from the fall, the animals jumped and clapped with joy, happy to have achieved something so difficult together. The whole day was spent partying.

The Martian observed everything, and when he returned to his planet the other Martians were *astonished* at what had happened. And so it was that those simple and helpful animals taught the Martians the importance of working together, joyfully, in a team. Since then, Martians no longer travel alone during their journeys through space. Now they go in groups, always willing to help each other, and make *sacrifices* whenever necessary.

叫，还有各种动物的哭喊声混合在一起。看到这一切，火星人以为动物们会非常生他的气，因为他们会把这一切都怪到他身上。

不过事实恰好相反。当动物们纷纷起身时，他们高兴得蹦蹦跳跳地鼓着掌，因为他们一起完成了一件如此艰难的事。他们一整天都在开派对庆祝。

火星人把一切都看在了眼里，当他回到火星后，其他火星人都为发生的事感到很惊讶。正是那些平凡而乐于助人的动物们教会了火星人高高兴兴团结合作的重要性。从那以后，火星人再也没有人独自在太空旅行。现在他们都是几个人结伴一起旅行，总是乐于帮助他人，并且会在必要时做出牺牲。

---

astonish *v.* 使十分惊讶   sacrifice *n.* 牺牲

8

Fiona Famous

Fiona Famous was a very *popular* girl
at school. She was clever and fun,
and got on well with everyone. It was no
accident that Fiona was so popular. From
an early age she had made an effort to be
kind and friendly to everyone. She invited
the whole class to her birthday party, and
from time to time she would give presents

菲奥娜·费默斯

菲奥娜·费默斯是一个在学校非常受欢迎的女孩，她既聪明又幽默，和每个人都相处得很愉快。菲奥娜如此受欢迎并非偶然。她从小就努力对每个人都很亲切和友好。她邀请全班同学参加她的生日聚会，还时不时地给每个人送礼物。她忙着跟许多人交朋友，结果几乎没有机会交到单个的朋友。不过她觉得很幸运，因为没有其他的女孩在学校里和

---

popular *adj.* 受欢迎的

to everybody. She was such a busy girl, with so many friends, that she hardly got a chance to spend time with individual friends. However, she felt very lucky; no other girl had so many friends at school and in the *neighbourhood* .

But everything changed on National Friendship Day. On that day, at school, everyone was having a great time, drawing, painting, giving gifts. That day in class everyone had to make three presents to give to their three best friends. Fiona enjoyed the task of choosing three from amongst all the dozens of her friends.

However, when all the presents had been made and shared out among classmates, Fiona was the only one who had not received a present! She felt terrible, and spent hours crying. How could it be possible? So much effort to make so many friends, and in the end no one saw her as their best friend? Everyone came and tried

---

家附近有那么多的朋友。

但是在国家友谊日那天，一切都改变了。那天，在学校每个人都玩得很愉快，他们画画、互相赠送礼物。当天，班级里的每个同学都要制作三份礼物，并且送给自己最好的三个朋友。菲奥娜很享受从她众多的朋友中挑选出三个的过程。

然而，当所有的礼物都准备好，并在同学之间分享之后，菲奥娜是唯一一个没有收到礼物的人！她很伤心，哭了好几个小时。怎么会这样呢？她那么努力地去结交那么多朋友，结果却没有一个人把她当成最好的朋

---

neighbourhood *n.* 邻近地区；所在地

to *console* her for a while. But each one only stayed for a short time before leaving.

This was exactly what Fiona had done so many times to others. She realised that she was a good *companion* and *acquaintance* , but she had not been a true friend to anyone. She had tried not to argue with anyone, she had tried to pay attention to everyone, but now she had found out that that was not enough to create true friendship.

When she got home that night, created quite a *puddle* with her tears, and Fiona asked her mother where she could find true friends.

"Fiona, my dear," answered her mother, "you cannot buy friends with a smile or a few good words. If you really want true friends, you will have to give them real time and affection. For a true friend you must always be available, in good times and bad."

友。大家都过来安慰了她一会儿。不过每个人都只待了一小会儿就走了。

其实菲奥娜很多次也是这样对待其他人的。她意识到，她是个很好的伙伴和熟人，却从不是任何人的真正朋友。她尽量不跟任何人争吵，并且尽量关心每个人，现在却发现这些都不足以建立真正的友谊。

当晚菲奥娜回到家以后，大哭了一场，她问妈妈在哪才能找到真正的朋友。

"菲奥娜，我的宝贝，"她妈妈回答道，"你无法用微笑或甜言蜜语来收买朋友。如果你真的想要真正的朋友，你就得真正花时间关心、爱护他们。对一个真正的朋友来说，不管他们身处顺境或逆境，你都必须要陪伴在他们左右。"

console *v.* 安慰；抚慰

acquaintance *n.* 熟人；相识的人

companion *n.* 同伴；伙伴

puddle *n.* 水洼，水坑

"But I want to be everybody's friend! I need to share my time among everyone!"Fiona protested.

"My dear, you're a lovely girl," said her mother, "but you can't be a close friend to everybody. There just isn't enough time to be available for everyone, so it's only possible to have a few true friends. The others will be *playmates* or acquaintances, but they won't be close friends."

Hearing this, Fiona decided to change her ways so that she could finally have some true friends. That night, in bed, she thought about what she could do to get them. She thought about her mother. Her mother was always willing to help her, she put up with all of Fiona's dislikes and problems, she always forgave her, she loved her a great deal... That was what makes friends!

And Fiona smiled from ear to ear, realising that she already had the best friend anyone could ever want.

"可是我想做每个人的朋友！我需要跟所有人在一起！"菲奥娜反驳道。

"宝贝，你是个很可爱的女孩，"她妈妈说，"但是你不可能成为所有人的密友。你没有那么多的时间去陪伴每一个人，所以你只能拥有少数几个真正的朋友。其他人会是你的玩伴或者熟人，却不可能成为你的密友。"

听到这些话，菲奥娜决定改变行事方式，好让自己最终能有一些真正的朋友。那天夜里，菲奥娜躺在床上，心想该怎样赢得真正的朋友。她想到了她的妈妈。她的妈妈总是愿意帮助她，妈妈容忍了她的讨厌之处和所有毛病，总是会原谅她，非常爱她……这才是朋友应该做的！

意识到自己已经拥有了一个人想要的最好的朋友，菲奥娜笑得都合不拢嘴了。

---

playmate n. 玩伴

9

The Unfriendly River

Once upon a time there was a river. This river was rather unfriendly and *lonesome*. The river could not remember how long ago he had decided that he no longer wanted to put up with anything or anyone. He lived alone, refusing to share his water with any fish, plant or animal.

And so his life went on, sadly and filled with *loneliness* , for many centuries.

不友好的小河

从前有一条小河，这条小河非常不友好且非常寂寞。他自己也记不清是什么时候决定，他再也不想容忍任何人或任何事了。他一个人生活着，拒绝跟任何鱼、植物或动物分享他的水。

他就一直这样过着日子，又伤心又孤单地度过了许多年。

---

lonesome *adj.* 寂寞的；孤独的   loneliness *n.* 孤独；寂寞

One day, a little girl with a goldfish bowl came to the bank of this river. In the bowl lived Scamp, her favourite little fish. The girl was about to move to another country, and she wouldn't be able to take Scamp with her. So she had decided to give Scamp his freedom.

When Scamp fell into the river, he immediately felt the river's loneliness. Scamp tried talking to the river, but the river told Scamp to go away. Now, Scamp was a very happy little fish, and he wasn't going to give up so easily. He asked and asked, swam and swam, and finally he started jumping in and out of the water. The river, feeling all the jumping and *splashing* , started to laugh. It tickled!

After a while, this put the river in such a good mood that he started talking to Scamp. Almost without knowing it, by the end of that day, Scamp and the river had become very good friends.

The river spent that night thinking about how much fun it was to

---

　　一天，一个小女孩拿着一个金鱼缸来到小河边。鱼缸里住着她最喜欢的一条小鱼斯坎普。女孩即将要搬到另一个国家去，她不能带斯坎普一起走，所以决定还斯坎普自由。

　　当斯坎普掉进水里时，他马上感觉到小河的寂寞。斯坎普试着跟小河说话，可是小河却让斯坎普走开。现在斯坎普是一条非常快乐的小鱼，他不会轻易地放弃的。他不停地问小河问题，不停地游啊游，后来开始在水里跳进跳出。小河感觉到了小鱼的跳跃和河水的飞溅，开始哈哈大笑。这让他感到很痒！

　　过了一会儿，小河开心的开始跟斯坎普说话了。不知不觉，到那天结束的时候，斯坎普和小河已经成了非常好的朋友。

---

splash *v.* 溅；拍打着水游

have friends, and how much he had missed by not having them. He asked himself why he had never had them, but he couldn't remember.

The next morning, Scamp woke the river with a few *playful* splashes... and that was when the river remembered why he had decided to be such an unfriendly river.

He remembered that he was very *ticklish* , and that he wouldn't have been able to stand it! Now he remembered perfectly how he had told everyone to *scoot* , that he wasn't going to put up with all that tickling.

But, remembering how sad and lonely he had felt for so many years, the river realised that although it may sometimes be a bit inconvenient or uncomfortable, it was always better to have friends and to try to be happy.

那天晚上，小河一直在想，有朋友的感觉真好，以及他以前因为没有朋友而错过了多少快乐。他问自己，为什么自己以前从来没有朋友，可是他怎么也想不起来了。

第二天早上，斯坎普顽皮地用水花把小河泼醒了……这时小河才想起来他当初为什么决定做一条不友好的小河。

他想起来了，他很怕痒，一点也忍受不了痒的感觉！现在他完全记起来，自己是怎样把大家都赶走的，他再也不想忍受那种痒的感觉。

但是，想起这么多年他是多么的伤心和寂寞，小河意识到，虽然有时候有点不便和不舒服，但有朋友和开心的感觉总是更好一些的。

---

playful *adj.* 闹着玩的；嬉戏的　　　　　　　ticklish *adj.* 怕痒的
scoot *v.* 疾行；匆匆离去

10

Looking Out the Window

Once upon a time there was a little boy who became very ill. He had to spend all day in bed, unable to move. Because other children weren't allowed to come near him, he suffered greatly, and spent his days feeling sad and blue.

There wasn't much he could do except look out of the window. Time passed, and his feeling of *despair* just grew. Until one

看看窗外

从前有一个小男孩，他病得很重。他每天只能躺在床上，一动也不能动。因为其他的孩子不被允许靠近他，他非常痛苦，整日愁眉苦脸、闷闷不乐。

除了看看窗外，他什么也做不了。随着日子一天天过去，他的绝望之感与日俱增。直到有一天，他看到窗户上有一个奇怪的形状。那是一只企

---

despair *n.* 绝望；失望

day he saw a strange shape in the window. It was a *penguin* eating a sausage sandwich. The penguin *squeezed* in through the open window, said "good afternoon" to the boy, turned around, and left again.

Of course, the boy was very surprised. He was still trying to work out what had happened, when outside his window he saw a monkey in a *nappy* , busy blowing up a balloon. At first the boy asked himself what that could possibly be, but after a while, as more and more crazy-looking *characters* appeared out the window, he burst out laughing and found it hard to stop.

Anyone wanting to stop laughing would never be helped by seeing a pig playing a tambourine , an elephant jumping on a trampoline, or a dog wearing a pair of glasses and talking about nothing except politics. The little boy didn't tell anyone about this because who would have believed him? Even so, those strange characters ended

---

鹅，正在吃香肠三明治。企鹅从开着的窗户挤进来，对男孩说了句"下午好"，然后就转身离开了。

小男孩当然非常吃惊，他还在想刚才到底发生了什么，这时他看见窗外有一只穿着尿布的猴子，它正在忙着吹气球。起初，男孩问自己那会是什么，但是过了一会儿，越来越多的长相疯狂的人物出现在窗外，他突然哈哈大笑起来，怎么也停不下来。

如果一个人想停止大笑，却看见一只猪在打手鼓，一头大象在玩蹦床，一条狗戴着一副眼镜大谈政治，那么他是无论如何也停不下来的。小男孩没有把这件事告诉任何人，因为有谁会相信他呢？即便如此，那些奇

---

penguin *n.* 企鹅

nappy *n.* 婴儿的围兜或纸巾；尿布

squeeze *v.* 挤入；挤过

character *n.* 人物

up putting joy back in his heart, and in his body. Before long, his health had improved so much that he was able to go back to school again.

There he got to talk to his friends, and tell them all the strange things he had seen. While he was talking to his best friend he saw something sticking out of his friend's school bag. The boy asked his friend what it was, and he was so *insistent* that finally his friend had to show him what was in the bag.

There, inside, were all the fancy-dress suits and *disguises* that his best friend had been using to try to cheer the little boy up!

And from that day on, the little boy always did his best to make sure that no one felt sad and alone.

怪的人物还是让小男孩重新快乐起来了。不久，他的身体好多了，他又能回学校上课了。

回到学校以后，他把看到的所有奇怪的事都告诉给他的朋友们了。当他跟最要好的朋友说话时，他看见朋友的书包里伸出一样东西。小男孩问朋友那是什么，因为他一直问个不停，朋友只好给他看了书包里的东西。

书包里面全是奇装异服和伪装饰品。他最好的朋友就是用这些来鼓励小男孩，让他快乐起来的。

从那天起，小男孩一直尽自己最大的努力，保证没有人感到悲伤和孤独。

---

insistent *adj.* 坚持的；固执的　　　　disguise *n.* 伪装物；化装用具

11

The Origin of Happiness

There was once a boy who hardly had any toys or money. *Nevertheless* , he was a very happy little boy. He said that what made him happy was doing things for others, and that doing so gave him a nice feeling inside. However, no one really believed him; they thought he was *loopy* .

He spent all day helping others,

快乐之源

从前有一个男孩，他几乎没有任何玩具，也没有一点儿钱。尽管如此，他却是个非常快乐的小男孩。他说让他高兴的事就是帮助他人，帮助他人让他从心里感到快乐。可是没有人真的相信他说的话，大家都觉得他是个疯子。

男孩每时每刻都在帮助别人，他为最贫穷的人提供施舍，还照顾被遗

---

nevertheless *adv.* 然而；尽管如此   loopy *adj.* 疯狂的；怪异的

dispensing charity to the poorest, and looking after *abandoned* animals. Very seldom did he ever do anything for himself.

One day, he met a famous doctor who thought the boy's case was so *peculiar* that he decided to *investigate* him. So, with a complex system of cameras and tubes, the doctor managed to record what was happening inside the boy. What he discovered was surprising.

Each time the boy did something good, a thousand tiny angels gathered around the boy's heart and started tickling it.

That explained the boy's happiness, but the doctor continued studying until he discovered that we all have our own thousand angels inside us. Unfortunately, he found that, as we do so few good things, the angels spend most of their time wandering about, bored.

弃的小动物。可他却极少为自己做点什么。

　　一天，男孩遇到一位有名的医生。这位医生觉得他非常特别，于是决定对他进行调查。所以，通过一套由摄像机和管子组成的复杂系统，医生设法记录下在男孩体内发生的事。结果他的发现让他惊讶万分。

　　每当男孩做一件好事时，就会有一千个小天使聚集在他的心脏周围，开始给它带来快乐。

　　这就解释了男孩快乐的原因，但是医生继续研究，后来他发现，我们每个人体内都有一千个天使。然而不幸的是，他发现，因为我们好事做得太少，这些天使大部分时间都在游荡，无聊至极。

---

dispense *v.* 提供；施予　　　　　　　abandoned *adj.* 被抛弃的
peculiar *adj.* 不寻常的；特殊的　　　investigate *v.* 调查；研究

And so it was that the secret to happiness was discovered. Thanks to that little boy we now know exactly what we have to do to feel our hearts being *tickled*.

就这样，人们发现了快乐的秘密。多亏了这个小男孩，现在我们终于知道，到底要怎样做才能从心里感到快乐。

---

tickle *v.* 使高兴；使满足

12

A Madman in the City

Julian finally left his village when there was no one left living there. He had never left his beloved village before, but *intrigued* by the fact that everyone had gone to the city, he decided to go and see for himself what wonderful things those cities had. So he packed a knapsack with a few clothes, put on his best smile, and off

---

城里的疯子

朱利安终于离开了村子，他走的时候村子里已经没有人了。他之前从来没有离开过他热爱的村庄，可是所有人都去城里了，这激起了他的好奇心，他决定也出去走走，亲眼看看那些城市里都有什么好东西。于是，他在背包里装了几件衣服、带着最灿烂的笑容，奔向了城

---

intrigue *v.* 激起好奇心

he went to the city.

On reaching the city, he was given a most unexpected welcome. A couple of policemen stopped Julian and questioned him in great detail. It turned out that Julian had seemed "*suspiciously* happy" for someone with hardly any possessions. In the end, the police had to let him go, but they were still suspicious about this apparently simple and good-natured fellow.

The first thing Julian noticed about the city was all the rushing around. Everyone was in such a hurry that he thought that there must be something special happening that day, which no one wanted to miss. Curious as to what it was, Julian started following a man who looked like he was hurrying to see whatever it was that was happening. However, after several hours following him, the man arrived at a small flat and went inside. He had done or seen nothing

市。

　　一到城市里，迎接他的是非常出人意料的事。两个警察拦住了朱利安，盘问了他很多细节问题。原来是因为朱利安作为一个几乎一无所有的人竟然这么开心，看上去太可疑了。最后，警察不得不放他走，但是他们还是对这个看起来单纯、温厚的家伙心存怀疑。

　　朱利安对城市的最初印象就是，周围的一切都很匆忙。所有人都在着急赶时间，所以他以为那天一定是有什么特别的事情发生，而且是所有人都不愿错过的事情。朱利安很好奇到底是什么事，就开始跟着一个行色匆匆的人，那人好像正在赶着去看什么事。然而，跟着他几个小时候后，这

suspiciously *adv.* 可疑地

of interest that whole day.

That night Julian slept in a park. The park was *strewn* with bits of paper and plastic. As the bins were completely empty, Julian thought how cool it was that the city had seemingly invented plants with *petals* made of paper and plastic. He only believed this until the following morning, when a man came by and dropped his chocolate wrapper.

Julian carried on walking through the city streets, trying to understand what was going on, when he arrived at a group of big *warehouses* , which many people were entering. "This must be the best museum in the world," he thought, on entering, and seeing all the useless-looking things they had inside. But then he saw that people were picking these things up, paying for them, and taking them away.

人来到了一个小公寓，然后就进去了。那一整天他都没有做任何事情，也没有看到任何有意思的事情。

那晚，朱利安睡在一个公园里。公园里布满着小片纸张和塑料。因为垃圾箱完全空着，朱利安就以为这个城市似乎是发明了纸和塑料作花瓣的植物，真是不赖。到了第二天早上，当他看到一个过路人随手扔掉巧克力包装纸的时候，他就不再那么想了。

朱利安继续穿行在城市的街道上，试着去了解发生在城市里的事情。当他来到一大片仓库跟前，看着好多人走进去，他想："这一定是世界上最好的博物馆。"他边想边走进去，他看到了里面所有的东西，看起来都没什么用处。可是随后他又看到人们在挑选这些东西，付钱买这些东西，然后把东西带走。

---

strew *v.* 撒满；布满

warehouse *n.* 仓库

petal *n.* 花瓣

"Why would anyone want a watch which doesn't show the minutes?" he wondered to himself, after seeing a woman very contentedly leaving with the most modern of watches on her wrist. He thought pretty much the same when seeing a pair of shoes with impossibly high heels, and then some electronic device which did a thousand things, and none of them well. Once again, he decided to follow the lady with the watch. He saw her joy turn into disappointment when her friends gave her new watch a look of *disapproval*. Julian started regretting having left his village, just to come to this place where no one seemed happy.

Then he saw a few kids playing. Now, they certainly did seem happy, playing, running about, chasing each other. Except for one child, who seemed troubled by a little machine they were calling

---

"为什么有人会要不能显示分针的手表？"看到一个女人腕上戴着最时髦的手表心满意足地离开，他不禁独自疑惑着。随后他又看到了一双有着奇高无比的鞋跟的高跟鞋，看到了一些会做各种事情、但是没有一件事做得好的电子设备，类似的疑惑又涌上心头。再一次，他决定跟着戴表的女士去看个究竟。他看到，当这位女士的朋友并不欣赏她的新手表时，她立刻由喜悦变为失望。朱利安开始后悔离开村子了，他离开村子来到的这个烂地方竟然没有一个人看起来是快乐的。

然后他看到了几个孩子在玩耍。此时此刻，他们看起来确实很开心，他们玩着，跑着，互相追逐着。只有一个孩子除外，那个孩子似乎被一个他们叫作"家用游戏机"的小机器困扰着。他用手指非常用力地敲打着

---

disapproval *n.* 不赞成；反对

a console. He was hitting it so hard with his fingers, and making all kinds of faces and angry gestures, that when one of the other children came over to invite him to play with them, the boy with the console just rudely walked away. Julian thought that the boy was trying to destroy that little machine because it was making him so unhappy. He decided to help the boy. Julian went over, took the console, threw it on the ground, *stamped* on it, and looked at the boy with great satisfaction.

At this the boy flew into a rage, as did all the other children there, and nearly all the adults. They pursued Julian so *relentlessly* that he had to run away. He didn't stop running until he reached the road leading back to his village.

As he was making his way home he couldn't help wondering whether the whole world had gone mad.

它，做出各种表情和生气的动作，甚至当一个孩子过来叫他和他们一起玩的时候，这个带着"家用游戏机"的孩子竟然粗鲁地走开了。朱利安以为那个男孩是想毁掉那个小机器，因为它让他太不开心了。他决定帮助男孩。朱利安走过去，拿起"家用游戏机"摔在了地上，并在上面踩了几脚，然后满意地看着那个男孩。

男孩暴怒，在那的其他孩子也都很生气，甚至是所有的大人都生气了。他们毫不留情地追赶着朱利安，他不得不跑走。他一直跑到了回村的路上才停下来。

他走在回家的路上，不禁疑惑，是不是整个世界都疯了呀。

---

stamp *v.* 重踩；重踏   relentlessly *adv.* 毫不留情地

13

The Happy Sweeper

A *loutish* kid and his mates were visiting a theme park. They arrived very early and everything was empty and clean. A park cleaner came by, singing and dancing as he swept. As everything was already so clean, the group of friends found it amusing to see how the cleaner worked so joyfully, and so early in the morning.

快乐的清洁工

一个粗野的孩子和他的同伴去参观一个主题公园。他们到的非常早，公园里空荡荡的，很干净。一个公园的清洁工从他们旁边经过，边唱边跳，边打扫着。因为公园里所有地方都已经非常干净了，这群朋友看着清洁工在清晨如此快乐地工作，感到很有意思。他们捉弄清洁

loutish *adj.* 粗野的

They had a great time making fun of him. But the cleaner didn't mind, and just kept sweeping the area clean.

So the *gang* started throwing bags and bits of paper on the ground, "to give him something to do". When more visitors started arriving, and saw the *lout* and his friends throwing litter about, they thought it was one of the park's fun activities. So they joined in, and as more people arrived, the park became covered in rubbish. The park cleaner couldn't *cope* . No one seemed to be bothered, but something strange started happening.

As time went on, the park attractions were emptying, and more people were looking down at the rubbish on the ground. By the end of the day no one was on any of the park rides; they were all standing about, looking at the ground. "Well," said the park *authorities* ,

---

工，玩得很痛快。但是清洁工并不在意，继续打扫着，把这块区域清理得干干净净。

于是，这伙人开始往地上扔袋子和碎纸片，按照他们的说法是"给他找点事情做"。越来越多的游客开始陆续来到公园，看到这个粗野的孩子和他的朋友们在四处扔垃圾，他们还以为这是公园的一项娱乐活动呢。所以他们也加入进来，随着公园里的人越来越多，整个公园最后被垃圾覆盖了。这个公园清洁工再也应付不过来了。似乎没有人因此感到困扰，但是奇怪的事情开始发生了。

随着时间的流逝，公园的景点都没什么人了，越来越多的人都低头看

---

gang *n.* 一伙人
cope *v.* 对付；处理

lout *n.* 举止粗野的男人或男孩
authority *n.* 当局；当权者

"what's going on here?"

Well... Everyone was looking for something!

It turned out that some time during that day, everyone had dropped something on the ground, but now that it was covered with litter, whenever anyone dropped anything, it was almost impossible to find it!

There was no other solution than have everyone help to clean the park, so they could find their things. *Encouraged* by the park cleaner, the visitors swept the ground, singing and dancing all the while. It became so much fun that from that day they created a new activity in the park, in which everyone, armed with brushes and bags, spent a while cleaning, laughing, and dancing.

着地上的垃圾。到晚上，公园的小路上一个人都没有，他们都站着，看着地面。"呦，"公园管理者说，"这儿发生了什么？"

唉……大家都在找东西呢！

原来在那天的某个时候大家都在地上掉了什么东西，可是现在地面都布满了垃圾，一旦有人掉了东西，几乎是不可能找到了！

想要找到他们的东西，除了大家一起帮忙打扫，没有别的解决办法了。受公园清洁工的鼓舞，游客们打扫起了地面，从始至终都边唱边跳着。真是太有趣了，从那天开始，他们在公园里创造了一项新活动，那就是大家都带着刷子和袋子打扫上一小会儿，开心地笑着，欢快地跳着。

---

encourage v. 鼓励；激励

14

Stickybeard's Treasure

According to *legend* , Stickybeard was the most sweet-toothed *pirate* who ever existed. He spent years *raiding* and *pillaging* sweetshops, and, so they say, he buried the greatest hoard of treasure any child could imagine, in some forgotten place. So when Tony and his friends found a strange old wooden chest, along with what seemed to be a treasure map for

斯蒂奇彼尔德的宝藏

根据传说，斯蒂奇彼尔德是有史以来最喜欢甜食的海盗。多年来他抢劫掠夺了许多糖果店，所以人们都说，他在某个被人遗忘的角落里埋藏了任何一个孩子都能想到的最棒的财宝。所以，当托尼和他的朋友们找到一个奇怪又古老的大木箱和一张在孩子看来是藏宝图的东西

legend *n.* 传说
raid *v.* 抢劫；劫掠

pirate *n.* 海盗
pillage *v.* 抢劫；掠夺

children, they were *understandably* excited. They readied themselves for the Great Stickybeard Treasure Hunt.

Off they went, and, following clues from the map, they arrived at a dark cave next to a lake. There they found another, smaller, chest. In it they found a few sweets, a big sign containing just the letter D, and another map with further *instructions* for finding the treasure. This helped the children get over the *initial* disappointment of realising they hadn't yet found the great treasure of Stickybeard. Tony and his friends took several days to *decode* the map, and had to consult quite a few books to manage it. It led them to a great big hollow tree, where, again, they found another chest containing some sweets, a new map, and a big letter O written on a piece of paper. And so they carried on, finding two similar chests with some sweets and the letters C and B. However, the last map they found was really strange. Rather than a map, it seemed more like a list of incomprehensible

的时候，他们当然兴奋极了。他们准备去寻找斯蒂奇彼尔德伟大的宝藏。

他们出发了，按照地图的指示，他们来到湖边一个黑暗的山洞。在那里他们又发现了一个小一点儿的箱子。里面装有一些糖果、一个只写有字母D的大标志，还有另一张地图。地图上面写着寻找宝藏的进一步说明。本来孩子们因为没有找到斯蒂奇彼尔德的伟大宝藏而失望，但是这些发现让他们重新燃起了希望。托尼和他的朋友们花了几天时间来破译地图，他们翻阅了好多书才破译了地图。地图指引他们找到了一棵中空的大树，在树里他们又发现了一个箱子，里面也装着糖果、一张新地图和一张写着大大的字母O的纸。他们继续寻宝，又发现了两个相似的箱子，里面还是装

understandably *adv.* 可理解地；合乎情理地　　instruction *n.* 指示；说明
initial *adj.* 开始的；最初的　　decode *v.* 破译；译解

instructions.

"You have the treasure in your mind,

It's something that you'll need to find,

A *portrait* painting once was done,

In which you see your granny's son,

And then I really think you ought to,

Place it by your granny's daughter,

Then you need to add the letters,

着糖果和写着字母C和B的纸。然而，他们发现的最后一张地图很奇怪。它不像是地图，更像是一张列出难以理解的指示的清单。

"宝藏就在你心中，

你只需要找到它。

画过一张肖像画，

里面有你的爸爸。

爸爸画像的旁边，

应该站着你妈妈。

收集所有的字母，

---

portrait *n.* 肖像；半身画像

Collected by you letter getters,

The secret will then be revealed,

That secret for so long concealed,

The one that brings your dreams much nearer,

The way to achieve them made much clearer."

They spent a long time arguing about the meaning of this puzzle, and the only thing they could agree on was that the riddle was talking about some paintings of a couple of parents. The rest remained a mystery. The discussions went on until, one day, they were talking about it in Tony's living room, staring *quizzically* at the letters they had collected. Alex, one of Tony's friends, looked at the

---

拼贴起来排一排。

秘密隐藏已许久，

此时此刻便揭开。

梦想终会变成真，

成功之门已敞开。"

他们就这个字谜的含义争论了好长时间，他们只在一个问题上看法一致，那就是，这个谜语说的是一对父母的肖像画。至于其他的意思，大家都没猜出来。讨论继续进行，直到有一天，他们在托尼家的客厅里谈论这

---

quizzically *adv.* 疑惑地

portrait of Tony's parents on the table, and suddenly he jumped up:

"I've got it!"

Everyone looked at him, quizzically, but instead of speaking, Alex went to the table. He *rearranged* the pieces of paper with the letters on them.

O...B...D...C

"Hey, Tony," said Alex, "Stickybeard was a Spanish pirate, wasn't he?"

"Yeah, he was... And?"

"Well, my mother is Spanish, and here's how they say those letters in Spanish..." everyone was looking at Alex with confused

---

个谜语，疑惑地盯着他们收集到的字母。托尼的朋友之一亚力克斯看着桌上放着的托尼父母的画像，突然跳了起来：

"我知道了！"

大家都疑惑地看着他。可是亚力克斯什么也没说，只是走到桌边，把带有字母的几张纸重新排序。

O……B……D……C

"嘿，托尼，"亚力克斯说道，"斯蒂奇彼尔德是个西班牙海盗，对吧？"

"是啊……怎么了？"

"我妈妈是西班牙人，这几个字母用西班牙语是这样说的……"大家

---

rearrange *v.* 重新排列

expressions, "Oh – Bay – Day – Say!"

"What?" asked Tony.

"In Spanish when you say the letters O, B, D, C it sounds like Oh - Bay - Day - Say... and that's the word 'obedece', which is Spanish for 'obey'. What Stickybeard was trying to say in his own language was 'Obey your parents'!"

"Obey your parents!" everyone shouted.

And even though there was no treasure *chest* filled with thousands of sweets, they were all willing to follow that great piece of advice. How could they not do so, when it came from someone like the famous Stickybeard?

都困惑地看着亚历克斯："偶——杯——的——斯！"

"什么？"托尼问道。"用西班牙语说OBDC这几个字母时，听起来就像'偶——杯——的——斯'，在西班牙语里是'服从'的意思。斯蒂奇彼尔德用西班牙语想表达的意思是'听父母的话'！"

"听父母的话！"大家喊道。

虽然没有装满几千块糖果的藏宝箱，他们也都愿意听从这条非常好的建议。当这句话是出自斯蒂奇彼尔德这样的名人之口时，他们怎么能不听呢？

---

chest *n.* （常为木制的）大箱子

15

Duck Race

Quick and Quack were two brave, *sporty* little ducks who lived with their mother. Both were really fast, and were always competing against each other. They raced each other in all sorts or places. On land, sea and air; running, swimming, or flying.

鸭子竞赛

奎克和夸克是两只勇敢又擅长运动的小鸭子，他们和妈妈一起生活。他们俩的速度都非常快，还常常互相比赛。他们在各种地方进行各种比赛：在陆地上赛跑，在海里比游泳，在空中比飞行。

---

sporty *adj.* 爱好（或擅长）体育运动的

One day, after visiting their Uncle Ducklass upriver, Quick shouted "last one home is a goose!" and both ducks swam quickly downriver. They both knew the way well, but Quack had been preparing a trick for some time. He had realised that the *current* in the middle of the river was stronger, and would help him. So, even though Mother Duck had told them never to swim in the middle of the river, Quack *paddled* over to it. "I'm old enough now to swim here," he thought to himself.

It wasn't long before he realised his mother had been right. He was going much faster than Quick, and was developing a big lead. Quick was not amused. He never disobeyed his mother, and now his obedience meant he was going to lose the race!

As they went on, the current got stronger. Quack *triumphantly*

一天，在拜访他们住在河上游的达克拉斯叔叔之后，奎克喊道"后到家的人是鹅！"于是两只鸭子开始迅速地向河下游游去。他们都很熟悉回家的路，但是夸克已经准备了一个诡计。他发现河中央的水流更急，这会让他游得更快。所以，虽然妈妈告诉过他们不要在河中央游泳，夸克还是游了过去。"我已经长大了，可以在这儿游了，"他心想。

很快夸克就意识到他妈妈说的是对的。他比奎克游得快多了，奎克被落下很远。奎克很不高兴。他从来没有不听妈妈的话，可是现在，听妈妈的话就意味着他要输掉这场比赛！

他们越往下游，水流越急。夸克得意扬扬地通过了终点线，却没发现

---

current *n.* 水流
triumphantly *adv.* 耀武扬威地；得意扬扬地
paddle *v.* 用脚或手轻轻划水

crossed the finishing line, without realising he was headed straight for a big *whirlpool* in the middle of the river. Before he could react, there he was spinning around in it, unable to escape.

Getting him out of there was no easy matter. No duck was strong enough to swim in those waters, and poor Quack kept *swallowing* water. The fact that his head was spinning like a top didn't help matters much either.

Fortunately, a cow from a nearby farm came by and, seeing Quack, *waded* in and rescued him, to prevent him from drinking all the water in the river. When he was on dry ground, he remained *dizzy* for quite some time. That provided quite a laugh for the various different animals that had been watching.

自己正在朝河中央的一个大漩涡游去。他还没反应过来，就被卷进去了，无法逃脱。

想把夸克从大漩涡里救出来可不是一件容易的事。没有哪只鸭子强壮得能在这样的漩涡中游泳。可怜的夸克不停地吞着河水。他的头像盖子一样旋转，一点作用也没有。

幸好附近农场的一只奶牛在此经过，看到了夸克，于是涉水去救他，他才不再喝河水了。当夸克被救上岸以后，他头晕了好长时间。这让围观的各种动物们大笑不止。

---

whirlpool *n.* 漩涡
wade *v.* 费力地走或过水、泥地等

swallow *v.* 吞下；咽下
dizzy *adj.* 眩晕的

That day, Quick understood that he had done well to listen to his mother, even though at first it might have seemed the difficult *option*. As for Quack... well... Quack could not forget that experience, even though he wanted to. From then on, whenever he touched a drop of water, he fell to the floor and spun round three times before being able to get up again. Rainy days proved quite *entertaining* !

那一天，奎克明白了自己听了妈妈的话是很正确的，尽管起初他并不情愿这么做。至于夸克，虽然他很想忘掉这次经历，可是怎么也忘不了。从那以后，每次他只要碰到一滴水，就会倒在地上转三圈，然后才能再站起来。一到下雨天就非常有趣啦！

option *n.* 选择   entertaining *adj.* 使人愉快的；有趣的

16

The Carnivorous Plant and the Butcher

Flora was a *carnivorous* plant, but truly in the meat-eating sense. She lived in a supermarket, next to her friend Porky the *butcher's* counter. Porky treated her with great *affection* and attention, and always had some *morsel* of meat to give her at the end of each day. But one day, Flora didn't get her ration of meat. Nor the next day,

食肉植物与屠夫

弗 洛拉是一株食肉植物，但她只是吃肉而已。她住在一家超市里，旁边就是她的朋友屠夫波奇的柜台。波奇对弗洛拉特别疼爱、特别关心，总是在每天结束的时候送给她一点儿肉。但是有一天弗洛

---

carnivorous *adj.* 食肉的
affection *n.* 喜爱；爱

butcher *n.* 屠夫
morsel *n.* 少量

and she got so worried that she decided to spy on Porky.

What she found out was that he wasn't giving her anything because he was putting lots of big *slabs* of meat in a big yellow box. *Pretending* not to know anything about it, Flora asked Porky if she could have a little of the food kept in the yellow box. He *responded* very *severely* that she could not, and added, "Don't even think about it, Flora! Don't ever think about touching the meat in that box."

The plant felt hurt, as well as hungry, and she couldn't stop wondering who Porky was keeping all that delicious-looking meat for. With her negative thoughts she was filling up with anger. That very night, when the shop was empty, she went over to the box, opened it, and ate that meat until her belly ached...

The next morning, when Porky arrived and discovered the theft , Flora felt terrible. He asked her several times whether she had taken

---

拉没有收到肉，第二天也没有收到。她非常担心，所以决定监视波奇。

弗洛拉发现，波奇什么也不给她是因为他把很多大块的肉都放到了一个黄色的大盒子里。她假装什么也不知道，问波奇能不能把黄色盒子里的食物给她一点儿。波奇很严肃地回答说不行，还说道："弗洛拉，你连想都不要想！千万别动这个盒子里的肉。"

弗洛拉感到很伤心，也很饿，她忍不住一直在想，波奇想把那些看起来很美味的肉留给谁呢？弗洛拉满脑子都是不好的想法，她越想越生气。当天晚上，当超市里空无一人的时候，她走到盒子旁边，打开盒子，开始吃起里面的肉来，一直吃到肚子疼……

第二天早上，波奇来到超市后发现肉被偷了，弗洛拉感觉很糟。波奇

---

slab *n.* 厚片；厚块
respond *v.* 回答；回应

pretend *v.* 假装；佯装
severely *adv.* 严肃地；严厉地

the meat. At first she denied it, but seeing Porky's worry and nerves she decided to *confess*.

"What have you done? You *reckless* thing!" Porky *exploded*, "I told you not to touch it! All that meat was poisoned!! That's why I haven't been able to give you anything for days. They sent us a *spoiled* delivery..."

Without delay, they found a Pharmabotanovet, with a Greenhouse-hospital, who managed to save Flora's life. She was already feeling great pain in her roots, and her leaves were changing colour. The shock hit everyone hard, but at least Flora learnt to stick to the rules set by those who most love us. That's much safer than just doing whatever you want.

问她是不是偷吃了盒子里的肉，他问了好几遍。起初弗洛拉一直不承认，但看到波奇既忧虑又紧张，便决定坦白。

"看你干的好事！你个鲁莽的家伙！"波奇大发雷霆，"我不是告诉你别动里面的肉了吗？！那些肉全是有毒的！！这就是我最近不能送肉给你的原因。他们给我们送来的是变质的肉……"

他们立刻找到了一位动植物医生，他有一所温室医院，挽救了弗洛拉的性命。弗洛拉当时已经感到自己的根部疼痛难忍，叶子也变了颜色。这件事让每个人都感到非常震惊，但至少让弗洛拉学会了一件事，那就是要遵守最爱我们的人所制定的规则。毕竟比起随心所欲来，这样更安全。

---

confess *v.* 坦白；承认
explode *v.* 勃然大怒；大发雷霆

reckless *adj.* 鲁莽的；不计后果的
spoiled *adj.* 变质的；腐败的

17

Bula the Traveller

Many years ago, a great lord called Bula recognised signs in the heavens; signs that had never been seen before. These *omens* announced the arrival of the greatest King the World would ever know. Amazed by the prospect of such power, the rich lord decided to set off in search of this King, intending to put himself

旅行者布拉

很多年以前，一个叫布拉的大贵族看到了上天的征兆——之前从没有看过的征兆。这些兆头预示着世界上有史以来最伟大的王者就要到来。这个富有的贵族对这种权力十分好奇，决定出发去寻找这个国王，打算为国王效力，以便在他将来的帝国里获取重要的职位。

他用所有的钱财组了一支旅行队前往神兆指示的地方。但是这个大贵

---

omen *n.* 预兆；征兆

at the King's service, and thus attain a position of importance in his future empire.

Gathering all his riches, he formed a great *caravan* and they moved off towards where the signs indicated. But the powerful lord didn't realise how long and hard the journey would be.

Many of his servants fell ill, and the good lord cared for them, expending great wealth on healers and doctors. They crossed such dry country that the inhabitants were dying of hunger, by the dozen. The lord allowed these people to join his *convoy*, and he provided them with food and clothing.

They met groups of slaves that were so terribly mistreated that the lord decided to buy their freedom, costing him great amounts of gold and jewels. The grateful slaves also joined Bula's party.

族并没有意识到这次旅途会有多么的艰辛漫长。

　　他的很多随从都病倒了，善良的贵族为了照顾他们，花了很多钱请医生、买药。他们穿过非常干旱的国家，当地的居民一批批地被饿死。这个贵族让这些人加入了他的旅队，给他们提供衣服和食物。

　　他们遇见了成群的被严重虐待的奴隶，贵族决定花钱买回他们的自由，这花掉了他一大笔金银珠宝。感激的奴隶们也加入了布拉的队伍。

caravan *n.* 旅行队　　　　　　　　　　　　convoy *n.* 车队；船队

So long was the journey, and so many people ended up joining the convoy, that when they finally arrived at their destination, only a small portion of the jewels were left, jewels that the lord had intended to be reserved as a gift for the great King. Bula then discovered the final sign: a great, shining star, rising up from behind some hills, and he headed towards it with the last of his riches.

He walked towards the great King's palace and came across many travellers, but against his expectations, few of them were noble, powerful people; most of them were shepherds, gardeners, and poor people. Seeing their *unshod* feet, and thinking of what little use such a powerful King would have for his few riches, Bula ended up sharing the last of his jewels with these poor people.

路途太长了，越来越多的人加入了旅队，当他们最后到达目的地的时候，只剩下一小部分珠宝了，那些珠宝原本是打算送给伟大的国王作礼物的。然后布拉发现了最后的征兆：一颗大大的闪耀的星星，从一些小山后面升起。于是他带着仅有的这些财富前往那个地方。

他向着伟大国王的宫殿走去，遇到了很多过路人。出乎意料的是，这些人里几乎没有体面、有实力的人；大多数都是牧羊人、园丁和穷人。看到他们连鞋都没有穿的脚，想到他剩下的那点珠宝对伟大的国王几乎没有什么作用，布拉把最后的这些珠宝也分给了这些可怜的人。

---

unshod *adj.* 没穿着鞋的

Without doubt, his plans had gone *awry*. Now he couldn't even apply for a position in the new Kingdom. Bula thought of turning around and going home, but he had been through so much to get there that he didn't want to leave without at least seeing the new King of the World.

So he carried on walking, and saw that after a bend the road came to an end. There was no sign of palaces, soldiers or horses. All he could see was a small stable at the side of the road, where a poor family were trying to protect themselves from the cold. Bula was disappointed at having got lost again, and he approached the stable, intending to ask these people if they knew the way to the new King's palace.

"I bring a message for him," he explained, showing them a *parchment* , "I would like to serve him and have an important position

---

毫无疑问，他的计划泡汤了。现在，他在这个新王国里甚至连一个职位都谋取不到了。布拉想过掉头回家，不过他毕竟经历了千辛万苦才到达这里，不想连新国王的面都没见上就离开。

所以，他继续前行，经过一个转弯看到了路的尽头。丝毫没有宫殿、士兵和马的影子。他能看到的只有路边的一个小马厩，马厩里有一家可怜的人在避寒。布拉又没有找对，他很失望。他走向马厩，打算问问那一家人是否知道去新王宫的路。

"我有信要给国王，"他解释道，给他们看了一张羊皮纸，"我想要替国王效力，在他的王国谋得一个重要的职位。"

---

awry *adv.* 出错；出岔子   parchment *n.* 羊皮纸

in his kingdom."

On hearing this, they all smiled, especially a newborn baby who was lying in a *manger*. The lady in the stable held out her hand and taking the message, said:

"Give me the message, I know him, and will give it him in person."

And she gave the parchment to the child who, to the sound of everyone's laughter, squashed it with his little hands and chewed it, putting the parchment beyond repair.

Bula didn't find this funny. Realising that he now had virtually nothing, he fell to the floor, crying bitterly. While he was weeping, the baby's hand touched his hair. The lord lifted his head and looked at the child. He was quietly smiling, and was such a lovely happy baby that Bula soon forgot his troubles and started playing with him.

听到这，他们都笑了，尤其是躺在食槽里新出生的婴儿笑得最厉害。马厩里的女士伸手去拿羊皮纸，说：

"把这个信给我，我认识他，我会亲自交给他的。"

然后她把羊皮纸给了这个孩子，孩子用小手把羊皮纸捏扁放到嘴里嚼起来，把它弄得不成样子，大家都笑了。

布拉并不觉得好笑。意识到他现在几乎是一无所有了，他倒在地上，失声痛哭起来。在他哭的时候，婴儿用手碰了碰他的头发。贵族抬起头看着孩子。他笑得非常开心，这样一个可爱快乐的婴儿让布拉很快忘记了烦恼，开始和他玩耍起来。

---

manger *n.* （牛、马的）食槽

And there he stayed, almost the whole night, in the presence of the poor family, telling them of his travels and adventures, and sharing with them what little he had left. When dawn broke, Bula got ready to leave, bidding farewell to all and kissing the baby. The child, smiling as he had done the whole night through, grabbed the *soggy* parchment and stuck it in Bula's face, making them all laugh. Bula took the parchment and kept it as a *souvenir* of that charming family.

That day he began his journey home.

Several days later, remembering his night in the stable, he found the parchment among his clothes, and opened it.

　　几乎整个晚上他都和这家可怜的人待在一起，给他们讲自己的旅行和冒险，并跟他们分享了自己剩下的东西。破晓的时候，布拉准备离开了，他向大家告别，并亲了那个婴孩。孩子笑着，他一整晚都笑着，他抓起湿乎乎的羊皮纸贴到布拉的脸上，弄得大家都笑了。布拉带走了羊皮纸，作为对这可爱的一家人的留念。

　　当天，他开始返程回家。

　　几天过后，布拉记起了在马厩的那天晚上，于是他在他的衣服里找到了那张羊皮纸，并打开了它。

---

soggy *adj.* 潮湿的　　　　　　　　　　　souvenir *n.* 纪念品；纪念物

The baby's *saliva* had left no trace of the original message. But right at that moment, while he was looking at the empty paper, fine drops of water and gold filled the air around the parchment and slowly came to rest on it. And with tears of happiness rolling down his cheeks, Bula read:

I received your message.

Thank you for coming, and for all the gifts you brought for my friends who you met on the way. I assure you, you already have a Great Position in my Kingdom.

Signed: Jesus, King of Kings

婴儿的唾液使原来的字迹都不见了。但是就在那时，在他看着这张空白的纸时，美妙的水珠和金星闪现在羊皮纸周围，慢慢落到纸上。布拉喜极而泣，泪水从脸颊流下，他读道：

我收到了你的来信。

感谢你的到来，感谢你送给我的朋友们的所有礼物，你在路上遇到的那些人都是我的朋友。我明确地告诉你，你已经在我的王国里有了崇高的位置。

落款：耶稣，万王之王

---

saliva *n.* 唾液

18

Bobby the Mountain Climber

Bobby the mountain climber was famous for his attempts to climb the big snowy mountain. He had tried it at least thirty times, but had always failed. He began the *ascent* at a good pace, focussing on the snowy summit, imagining the marvellous view and the sense of freedom up there. But as he went on, and

登山者鲍比

大家都知道登山者鲍比尝试攀登一座大雪山的壮举。他已经试过不下三十次了，可是总是失败。他刚开始爬的时候速度很不错，盯着白雪覆盖的顶峰，想象着到达峰顶时的非凡景象和自由的感觉。但是随着他爬得越来越高，体力也越来越少。他的目光会放低，更多的时

---

ascent *n.* 攀登

MCGRAW-HILL

his strength *dwindled* , his gaze would lower, and more often would he look at his worn out boots. Finally, when the clouds had gathered round him, and he understood that he wouldn't be able to enjoy the view from the summit that day, he would sit down to rest, relieved to be able to start the descent back down to the village, though slightly worried about all the jokes he would have to endure.

On one of these occasions he went up the mountain accompanied by old Peeper, the town *optician* , who bore witness to the failure. It was Peeper who most encouraged Bobby to try again, and he presented him with a pair of special sunglasses.

"If it starts clouding over, put these glasses on, or if your feet start hurting put them on too. These are special glasses; they'll help you."

候会看着他磨坏的靴子而不是山峰。最后，当他身边聚拢起云朵，他知道这一天他不可能在峰顶享受美景了，便坐下来休息，尽管还有小小的担忧，他没能爬上山，别人定是会取笑他的，但一想到可以开始下山回到村子里便松了一口气。

有一次，他和镇子里的眼镜商老敝伯一起去爬山，他亲眼看着鲍比没能登上峰顶。敝伯鼓励鲍比再试一次，并送给他一副特殊的太阳镜当作礼物。

"如果天空开始布满乌云，带上眼镜，或者如果你开始觉得脚疼，也要把眼镜戴上。这是特殊的眼镜，能够帮助你。"

dwindle *v.* 减少

optician *n.* 眼镜商

Bobby accepted the gift without giving it much mind, but when his feet started hurting again he remembered what Peeper had said, and he put on the glasses. The pain was pretty bad, but with those new sunglasses he could still manage to see the snow-covered summit; so on he continued.

Just as nearly always seemed to happen, misfortune returned in the form of cloud cover. But this time it was so light that he could still see the summit through the clouds. And so Bobby kept climbing, leaving the clouds behind, forgetting his pain, and finally arriving at the summit. It was certainly worth it. His feeling of triumph was incomparable; almost as magnificent as that wonderful view, *resplendent* in its silence, the mountain below surrounded by a dense sea of clouds. Bobby didn't remember the clouds being as thick as that, so he looked more closely at the sunglasses, and understood everything.

鲍比接受了礼物，没太在意，但是当他的脚再次疼起来的时候，他想起了㪚伯告诉他的话，于是戴上了眼镜。脚疼得很厉害，可是戴着这个新的太阳镜，他仍然可以看到白雪皑皑的峰顶，所以他继续攀登着。

像往常一样，不幸的事情又发生了，周围开始布满了云。可是这次云朵很薄，他仍然可以透过云看到峰顶。就这样，鲍比继续爬着，把云甩在了后面，忘记了疼痛，最后他终于到达了山顶。这一切都太值得了。他胜利的喜悦是不可比拟的；就像这美妙壮观的风景一样无与伦比，一切是那么的寂静而绚丽，山下环绕着密密的云海。鲍比之前并没觉得云朵有这么厚，他仔细地看看太阳镜，一切都明白了。

---

resplendent *adj.* 华丽灿烂的

Peeper had *engraved* a light image on the lenses, in the form of the snow-covered summit. It was made in such a way that you could only see it if you looked upwards. Peeper had understood that whenever Bobby lost sight of his objective, he would similarly lose sight of his dream, and his will to continue would *wane* .

Bobby realised that the only obstacle to reaching the summit had been his own *discouragement* . When he could no longer see the top of the mountain, the problems had set in. He thanked Peeper for using that little trick to help him see that his aims were not impossible, and that they were still there, where they had always been.

　　敝伯在镜片上轻轻地刻上了一个图案，那就是白雪覆盖的山顶。戴着这副眼镜，只有当你向上看的时候才能看到这个图案。敝伯明白一旦鲍比看不到目标，他就可能同样地看不到梦想，继续下去的决心便会变弱。

　　鲍比意识到阻碍他到达顶峰的不是别的，正是他自己的气馁。当他再也看不到山顶的时候，问题就出现了。他感谢敝伯用微妙的方法帮他看清了他的目标并不是不可实现的，目标仍然在那里，一直都在那里。

---

engrave *v.* 雕刻　　　　　　　　　　　　　wane *v.* 变小；变弱
discouragement *n.* 气馁

Friends from the Vegetable Patch

Lulu and Lily were two *spinach* plants who were born on the same vegetable patch. They had been friends all their lives. Together they had endured terrible frosts, snowstorms, and *scorching* hot summer days. Through it all they had always supported each other, looking forward to the time every spinach plant dreams of: the moment they are served

蔬菜地里的朋友

露露和莉莉是两棵生在同一块菜地里的菠菜。她们已经做了一辈子朋友了。她们一起经历了可怕的霜冻、暴雪和酷热的夏日。她们一直相互支撑着经受一切，期待着所有菠菜向往的那一天：有朝一

---

spinach *n.* 菠菜   scorching *adj.* 酷热的

on a child's dinner plate, the moment they get to pass on all their gathered strength.

So when harvest time arrived, Lulu and Lily were happy at being sent together to the spinach preparation factory, and then on to the packaging company and to the supermarket. At the supermarket they sat together, displayed on one of the very best shelves. They were both excited to see ladies passing by with their baskets. They were especially thrilled when any lady with a child came *nearby*. A whole day passed without anyone showing any interest in them, but just before closing time, a lady walked too close to their shelf, and without realising, knocked Lulu off the shelf. Lulu fell to the floor, right in front of the lady, and the lady's foot kicked Lulu under the stack of shelves.

No one realised what had happened, and Lulu spent the whole night crying, knowing that she would be left under the shelves

日，她们会在小孩子的餐盘里，把她们积蓄的力量传递下去。

所以，在丰收的时候，露露和莉莉很开心，她们被一起送到了菠菜加工厂，然后送到了包装公司，最后是超市。在超市里最好的一个架子上，她们被摆放到了一起。她们俩看到女士们拿着篮子从身旁经过都很兴奋。尤其是看到带着小孩的女士在附近便会格外兴奋。一整天过去了，没有一个人对她们感兴趣，可就在关店前，一位女士从她们所在的架子旁边走过，因为靠得太近了，她不小心把露露从架子上碰了下来。露露掉到地上，正掉到女士面前，她的脚又把露露踢到了这堆架子下面。

没人发现都发生了什么，露露哭了一整晚，她知道她也许就要在架子下面一直待到发霉烂掉了。莉莉非常担心，很遗憾她朋友的运气那么差，

nearby *adv.* 在附近

until she *moulded* away. Lily, very upset, regretted her friend's bad luck, but was unable to do anything. The next day, a lady with an adorable little boy seemed like she was going to buy Lily, but this did not cheer Lily up. She was thinking about her poor friend. In what was both a moment of madness and a moment of true friendship, she made one last attempt to help her lifelong friend. Just as the boy was about to grab Lily from the shelf, Lily threw herself to the floor and rolled under the shelves, ending up next to Lulu. The boy, surprised and amused, bent down and, without knowing it, picked up both Lulu and Lily.

Lily ended up with a pair of broken *stalks* , but it was a price worth paying to save her friend. And some hours later, sitting on a plate at Lulu's side, she felt like the happiest piece of spinach in the world, for managing to fulfill her dream alongside her best friend.

可是却无能为力。第二天，一位女士和一个可爱的小男孩似乎想要把莉莉买走，可是这并没有让莉莉开心起来。她正想着她可怜的朋友。这是一个鉴证友情的疯狂时刻，莉莉决定做最后的一次尝试去帮助她一辈子的朋友。就当男孩要从架子上抓起她时，她纵身落到了地上，滚到了架子下，正巧来到了露露身旁。男孩很吃惊，感到很有意思，他弯下腰，并非有意地把露露和莉莉她们两个都捡了起来。

结果莉莉弄断了几根梗，可是能够救出她的朋友还是值得的。几小时后，在一个盘子里，当莉莉躺在露露身边时，她感觉自己是世界上最快乐的一颗菠菜，因为她终于可以和她最好的朋友一起实现梦想了。

---

mould *v.* 发霉 　　　　　　　　　　　　　　　　stalk *n.* 梗

20

The Young Puppet-maker

There was once a young man who liked puppets so much that he became an *apprentice* to a master puppet-maker. Sadly, the young man was very *clumsy* , and his teacher and the other apprentices were always telling him he had no ability when it came to making puppets, and that he would never amount to anything.

年轻的木偶匠

从前有一个年轻人非常喜欢木偶，所以他成了一位木偶制作大师的徒弟。 可悲的是，年轻人非常笨，他的师傅和其他的学徒总是一直对他说，他是不可能制作木偶的，他不会做成任何事。

apprentice *n.* 学徒   clumsy *adj.* 笨拙的

Even so, he enjoyed it so much that he worked day after day to improve. Despite his efforts, they would always find something wrong with the puppets he had made, and they ended up throwing him out of the *workshop*.

He wasn't going to give up, so the young man decided that from then on he would spend all his time making just one kind of puppet. On he went, and whenever he found a fault in his puppet he would *abandon* it and start again right from square one. The years passed, and with each new attempt his puppet became a little bit better. By now, his puppet was much better than anything his old fellow apprentices could make, but he kept making improvements, seeking perfection. Living like that, the man wasn't making any money, and many people laughed at how poor he was.

　　尽管如此，可他是那么喜欢木偶，所以他日复一日地练习着，慢慢提高改进。尽管他很努力，可他做的木偶还是经常被别人挑出毛病，最后他被赶出了作坊。

　　年轻人并不打算放弃，所以他决定从那时开始，要用他所有的时间只制作一种木偶。他就这样继续着，每当他发现他的木偶有任何瑕疵，他都会把它扔掉重做。一年年过去了，随着他的每一次新的尝试，他的木偶都会有一点进步。到现在，他的木偶比他当年任何一个同伴学徒做的都要好。可是他还在继续提高，追求完美。他就这样地生活着，没有任何收入，许多人都笑话他，因为他太穷了。

---

workshop *n.* 作坊　　　　　　　　　　　　　abandon *v.* 抛弃

By the time he was an old man, his puppet was truly wonderful. So much so, that finally one day, after so many years of work, he finished work on his puppet, and said: "I can't find anything wrong with it. This time it is perfect," and for the first time in all those years, instead of abandoning his puppet, he put it up on the shelf, feeling truly satisfied and happy.

And the rest is history.

That perfect puppet came to life, had a thousand adventures, and gave that old man — whose name was *Geppetto* — more joy than any other famous puppet-maker ever got from any of their creations.

等他成为一个老人的时候，他的木偶真的棒极了。在这么多年的努力之后，终于有一天，他完成了他的木偶，说："我找不到它一丁点儿毛病。这次它真的完美了。"这些年来第一次，他没有扔掉木偶，而是把它放到了架子上，感到由衷地满足和快乐。

剩下的就是你知道的故事了。

那个完美的木偶活了，经历了许许多多的奇遇，给这位老人带来了很多快乐，任何其他著名的木偶匠都没能从他们创作的木偶那里得到过这么多的快乐，这位老人的名字叫盖比特。

Geppetto *n.* 盖比特（著名童话故事《木偶奇遇记》中的木匠，他制作的小木偶匹诺曹一说谎话鼻子就会变长，是全世界有名的经典童话人物）

21

The Photographic Elephant

There was once an elephant who wanted to be a photographer. How his friends would laugh when they heard him talk about it!

"How *silly* ," said some. "There aren't any cameras for elephants!"

"What a waste of time," others would

大象摄影师

从前有一只大象，他想当一名摄影师。他的朋友们听到他谈及此事都会大笑。

"多蠢呀，"有些人说。"根本就没有给大象使用的照相机！"

"多浪费时间呀，"其他人会这么说。"这里根本就没有可以拍照的东

---

silly *adj.* 愚蠢的

say. "There's nothing to photograph here anyway..."

But the elephant kept following his dream, and, piece by piece, he managed to *cobble* together some old bits of junk and some spare parts, and ended up with a camera of sorts. With this camera, the elephant had to design practically everything himself, from a button he pressed with the end of his trunk, to a lens made to fit an elephant's eye, to a load of wrought iron used to make a frame so the elephant could attach the camera to his head.

When it was all finished, he could finally get to taking his first photos. However, the elephant camera was so enormous and strange-looking that it seemed like some huge *ridiculous* mask. So many people laughed as he went by that the elephant began to think of abandoning his dream... Even worse, it was beginning to look like those who had said there was nothing to photograph there had been

---

西……"

可是大象继续追寻着他的梦想，他一点点地粗糙地组装起废品和旧零件，最后马马虎虎地做出一个相机。用这样一个相机，大象必须亲自设计几乎所有的东西，从可以用他的鼻尖触碰的按钮，到适合他眼睛的镜头，再到一堆用来做框架的熟铁，这样他就可以把相机戴到头上了。

一切都完工后，他终于可以开始照第一批相片了。然而，这个大象相机太大了，看起来非常奇怪，就像滑稽的大面具。所以，每当大象从人们身旁走过，许多人都会大笑，弄得大象开始想要放弃他的梦想了……更糟糕的

---

cobble *v.* 粗制滥造   ridiculous *adj.* 滑稽可笑的

right...

But things worked out differently. The sight of the elephant walking about with the camera on his head was so funny that no one could help but laugh when they saw him. And, using a great deal of good humour, the elephant managed to take some really amusing, incredible pictures of all the animals. In his photos they always looked joyful; even the moody *rhino*! So the elephant managed to become the official *savannah* photographer, and animals would come from every direction to have some nice photos taken for their passport to the zoo.

是，貌似那些说过那里根本没什么可以拍照的东西的人说得没错……

可是事情发生了转变。大象带着相机走来走去，这情景太好笑了，看到他的人都会忍不住大笑起来。大象运用了很多幽默元素，给所有动物都照了一些非常有趣、不可思议的照片。在这些照片里，他们看起来总是一副非常高兴的样子，就连喜怒无常的犀牛都不例外！所以大象成了大草原的官方摄像师，动物们都会从四面八方赶来拍去往动物园的护照上的照片。

rhino *n.* 犀牛

savannah *n.* 无树大草原

22

The Paper Rocket

There was once a boy whose greatest dream was to have a rocket, and launch it to the moon. Unfortunately, he had little money and couldn't afford one. One day, at the side of a path, he found a box for one of his favourite kinds of rocket. Opening it, he found there was only one rocket inside, made of *dodgy* paper, the

纸火箭

从前有个男孩，他最大的梦想就是能有一支火箭，并把它升上月球。不幸的是，他没什么钱，买不起火箭。一天，他在路旁发现一个他最喜欢的那种火箭的盒子。打开盒子，里面只有一支火箭，还是

dodgy *adj.* 有毛病的；状况不佳的

consequence of a factory *malfunction* .

The boy was very disappointed, but at least he now finally had a rocket of sorts. He started preparing his plans for the launch. For many days he collected paper of all shapes, sizes and colours; and with all his soul he set about drawing, painting, cutting, sticking, and colouring all the stars and planets that would turn his rocket into an outer space in paper form.

It wasn't an easy job, but the final result was so magnificent that his bedroom wall looked like an open window onto the *galaxy* . From then on, the boy enjoyed playing with his paper rocket every day. One day, a friend came to visit, and in the boy's bedroom he saw that spectacular sight. The friend offered to *swap* it with the boy, for a real rocket he had at home.

用质量很差的纸做成的，是工厂的残次品。

男孩非常失望，可是至少他现在终于马马虎虎算是有一个火箭了。他开始准备起升空计划了。他花了好多天收集了各种形状、各种大小和各种颜色的纸；然后全身心地开始绘画、剪裁、粘贴、上色，做出了很多小星星和行星，它们可以让它的火箭飞进纸质的外太空。

这并不是一件容易的事，可是最终的结果真是好极了，他卧室的墙面就像敞开的通往银河的窗户。从那时候起，男孩每天都很快乐地玩着他的纸火箭。一天，他有一个朋友过来玩，他的朋友看到了男孩卧室里的壮观景象，提出来要用一个他在家里的真火箭交换男孩卧室里的这些东西。

---

malfunction *n.* 故障   galaxy *n.* 银河
swap *v.* 交换

The boy went almost mad with joy, and delightedly accepted the swap. Since then, each day, playing with his new rocket, the boy would miss more and more his old paper rocket, with its planets, stars and all the rest. Really, he had much preferred playing with that one. He realised that it was much more fun playing with toys he had made himself, with great effort and *enthusiasm* .

And so it was, that the boy started building all his toys by himself, and when he grew up he became the greatest toy-maker in the whole world.

男孩开心极了，很高兴地接受了这个交换条件。从那以后，男孩每天玩着他的新火箭，都会越来越想念他的旧火箭，还有它的行星、小星星和其他的一切。其实，他还是更喜欢玩那支火箭。他意识到，自己付出很大的努力和热情亲手做的玩具玩起来要有意思得多。

确实是这样，男孩开始亲自制作他所有的玩具，长大后，他成了世界上最了不起的玩具制作师。

enthusiasm *n.* 热情

23

The Drawing That Talked

Pinty Tailor was a little boy who enjoyed going to school and doing all sorts of things, except for art and writing. Using *brushes* and pencils did not come easy to Pinty, so his works of art did not end happily, and he would just give up

---

会说话的图画

佩迪·泰勒是个喜欢上学的小男孩，他喜欢做各种各样的事情，除了绘画和写作。刷子和铅笔对佩迪来说真的不怎么好用，所以他每次画画都没能善始善终，总会很厌烦地半途而废。

---

bnush *n.* 刷子

in *disgust* .

But one day Pinty found a pencil of such lovely colours that he could not *resist*, and he tried drawing a circle. As ever, it did not go well, and he was about to throw the pencil away when his drawing began to speak to him.

"Psst! You aren't going to leave me like this, are you? Come on, the least you can do is draw me a pair of eyes!" said the drawing. Pinty was understandably shocked, but he managed to draw two little spots inside the circle.

"Much better, now I can see myself," said the circle, looking around at itself... "Arghh! But what have you done to me?! "

"I don't draw very well," said Pinty, trying to make excuses.

可是有一天，佩迪发现了一支颜色非常漂亮可爱的铅笔，他简直无法抗拒，于是就试着画了一个圆。和往常一样，画得并不好，他正要把铅笔扔掉，可他的画就在这时开始和他说话了。

"喂！你不会打算就这么扔下我吧，啊？快，至少你可以给我画双眼睛吧！"图画说。佩迪当然被吓了一跳，可他还是在圆里面画了两个小点。

"好多了，现在我可以看到自己了，"那个圆打量了一下自己说……"啊！你都对我做了什么？！"

"我没有画好，"佩迪试着找借口说。

---

disgust *n.* 反感；厌恶

resist *v.* 抵抗

"OK, no problem," the drawing interrupted him, "I'm sure that if you try again you'll do better. Go on, *rub* me out!" So Pinty *erased* the circle and drew another one. Like the first one, it was not very round.

"Hey! You forgot the eyes again!"

"Oh, yeah."

"Hmmm, I think I'm going to have to teach you how to draw until you can do me well," said the circle with its quick, *squeaky* little voice.

To Pinty, who remained almost *paralysed* with shock, this did not seem like a bad idea, and he immediately found himself drawing and erasing circles. The circle would not stop saying "rub this out, but carefully; it hurts," or "draw me some hair, quickly, I look like a lollipop !" and other funny remarks.

"好吧，没问题，"图画打断他说。"我相信再画一遍的话你会画得更好。继续，把我擦掉！"于是佩迪把圆圈擦掉又画了另一个。还是和第一个一样，没有画圆。

"嘿！你又忘了画眼睛了！"

"哦，还真是。"

"嗯，我想，我要教你怎么画画，一直到你把我画好了，"圆圈用它尖尖的声音急促地说。

佩迪还是被惊得呆呆的，没有缓过神来。对他来说，这主意貌似并不坏，他随即动手，一会儿画圆，一会儿擦掉……圆圈不停地说"擦掉，不过要小心，疼啊，"或者说"给我画点头发，快点，我看起来像根棒棒糖！"还有好多其他有意思的话。

---

rub *v.* 擦；摩

squeaky *adj.* 短促尖声的

erase *v.* 擦掉或刮掉

paralysed *adj.* 惊呆的

After spending nearly the whole afternoon together, Pinty could already draw the little figure much better than most of his classmates could have. He was enjoying it so much that he did not want to stop drawing with this crazy new teacher of his.

Before going to bed that night, Pinty gave his new *instructor* a hearty thank you for having taught him how to draw so well. "But I didn't do anything, silly!" answered the little drawing, in its usual quick manner.

"Don't you see that you've been practicing a lot, and enjoying it all the while? I bet that's the first time you've done that!"

Pinty stopped to think. The truth was that previously, he had drawn so badly because he had never practiced more than ten minutes at a time, and he had always done it angrily and *grudgingly*. Without doubt, what the little drawing had said was correct.

他们一起待了将近整个下午，一下午后，佩迪已经可以把这个小人画得比他大部分同学画过的都好了。他太高兴了，丝毫不想停笔，和他这位不可思议的新老师一起不停画着。

那晚，在上床睡觉之前，佩迪由衷地感谢了他的新老师让他学会了如何把画画得这么好。"可是我并没有做什么呀，傻瓜！"这个小图画用它一贯的急促腔调回答。

"你没发现吗？你练习了好多次，整个过程都很快乐。我敢打赌，你是第一次那么做！"

佩迪停下来想了想。其实，他之前之所以画得那么糟糕是因为他从没有一次练习超过十分钟，他总是不情愿地边画着边生气。毫无疑问，这个小图

---

instructor *n.* 指导者   grudgingly *adv.* 不情愿地

"OK, you're right, but thank you anyway," said Pinty, and before he went to bed he carefully placed the pencil in his school bag.

The next morning Pinty jumped out of bed and went running to find his pencil, but it was not there. He searched everywhere, but there was no sign of it. And the *sheet* of paper on which he had drawn the little figure, although still full of rubbing out marks, was completely *blank*. Pinty began to worry, and he did not know if he had really spent the previous afternoon talking with the little man or whether he had dreamt the whole thing.

So, to try to *settle* the matter, he took a pencil and some paper and tried to draw a little man.

画说的是正确的。

　　"好吧，你是对的，但还是要谢谢你，"佩迪说。上床之前，他小心翼翼地把那支铅笔放进书包里。

　　第二天早上佩迪跳下床，跑过去找他的铅笔，可是铅笔已经不在那里了。他找遍了每个地方，可是到处都不见它的影子。那张他画小人的纸完全是空白的，尽管上面满是擦掉的画痕。佩迪开始担心起来，他不知道他昨天是真的和那个小人说了一下午的话，还是这整件事情都是他做的梦。

　　于是，为了弄清楚是怎么一回事，他拿起一支铅笔和几张纸，尝试着画了一个小人。

---

sheet *n.* 一张　　　　　　　　　　　　　　　　blank *adj.* 空白的
settle *v.* 解决；了结

It turned out not bad at all, except for a couple of *jagged* lines. He imagined his *bossy* little teacher telling him to round out those edges, and that it looked like he was trying to give him spots. Pinty gladly rubbed out those bits and redrew them. He realised that the crazy little teacher had been right: it made no difference whether you had the *magic* pencil or not; to manage to do things, you only needed to keep trying and to enjoy doing so.

From that day on, whenever Pinty tried to draw or paint, or do anything else, he always had fun imagining the result of his work protesting to him and saying, "Come on, my friend, do me a bit better than that! I can't go to the party looking like this!"

　　然而除了几条毛糙的线之外，结果一点都不坏。他想象着他那爱发号施令的小老师正告诉他好好完成这些线，想象着他正试图指点他。佩迪很高兴地擦掉了那些小毛糙，重新来画。他意识到这个不可思议的小老师是对的：是否有魔法铅笔并不重要，要做成事情，你只需要不停地尝试和享受其中的快乐。

　　从那天起，每当佩迪要绘画或做其他事的时候，他总是快乐地想象着他的劳动成果对他提出抗议，说："快，我的朋友，把我弄得比这再好一些吧！这个样子我可没法去参加派对！"

---

jagged *adj.* 边缘不整齐的　　　　　　　　bossy *adj.* 爱发号施令的
magic *adj.* （似）用魔法变成的

24

Drums in Space

Brenda Bongos was a happy, artistic
girl, a girl with one big *ambition*—to
play the drums in a band. But one big
obstacle lay in her way. To be good enough
to play in a band Brenda had to practice
a lot, but she lived next-door to a lot of
old people—many of them sick—in a care
home. She knew that the sound of beating

太空中的鼓声

布伦达·邦戈是个有艺术天分的快乐小姑娘，她有一个很大的志
向，那就是在乐队里做鼓手。可是一个巨大的障碍横在她的面
前。想要做乐队鼓手，就必须要经常练习，鼓要敲得足够好才行，但是她
的隔壁是一个护理中心，里面住着很多老人，还有好多生病的。她知道，

---

ambition *n.* 志向

drums and crashing *cymbals* would really get on their nerves.

Brenda was a very good, respectful girl. She always tried to find a way of practicing her drums without bothering other people. So, she had tried playing in the strangest places: a basement, a kitchen, an attic, and even in a shower. But it was no good; there was always someone it would annoy. However, determined to practice as much as she could, Brenda spent most of her time playing on books and boxes, and looking for new places to practice.

One day, while watching a science documentary on TV, she heard that sound cannot travel in space, because there's no air. At that moment, Brenda Bongos decided to become a sort of musical astronaut.

With the help of a lot of time, a lot of books, and a lot of work,

---

敲锣打鼓的声音会让他们心烦的。

布伦达非常善良懂事。她总是试图找到一个可以不打扰他人的练鼓方法。于是，她试过在非常奇怪的地方打鼓：地下室，厨房，阁楼，甚至是在浴室。可是并不如意，总是有人会觉得烦。然而，布伦达已经决定了要尽可能多地练习，她大部分时间都在书本和盒子上敲着，一直寻找着新的练习场所。

一天，她正在电视上看一个科教纪录片，她听到上面说声音无法在太空中传播，因为太空中没有空气。就在那时，布伦达·邦戈决定成为一个特殊的音乐宇航员。

布伦达花了很多时间，读了很多书，做了很多工作，这一切帮助她打造

---

cymbal *n.* 铜钹

Brenda built a space bubble. This was a big glass ball connected to a machine which sucked out all the air inside. All that would be left inside was a drum kit and a chair. Brenda got into the space suit she had made, entered the bubble, turned on the machine, and...

She played those drums like a wild child!

It wasn't long before Brenda Bongos—"The Musical Astronaut"— had become very famous. So many people came to see her play in her space bubble that she had to mount a pair of speakers so that everyone could listen to her play. Shortly afterwards she came out of the bubble and started giving *concerts* . Her fame spread so much that the government proposed that she form part of a unique space journey. Finally, Brenda was a real musical astronaut, and had gone

---

了一个太空气泡。这是一个很大的玻璃球，连接着一个机器，这个机器是用来抽光里面的空气的。里面就只剩下一套鼓和一把椅子。布伦达穿上了自制的宇航服，进入了气泡里，开启机器，然后……

她像一个疯掉的孩子一样疯狂地打着鼓！

不久后，"音乐宇航员" 布伦达·邦戈变得非常有名。好多人都来看她在她的太空气泡里面表演，她要再加上一对儿喇叭才能让大家听到她的鼓声。很快，她就走出了气泡开始在音乐会上表演了。她的名气传播得很快，甚至连政府都提议她应该打造出独特的太空旅行。最后，布伦达成为了一名

---

concert *n.* 音乐会

far beyond her first ambition of playing drums in a band.

Years later, when they asked her how she had achieved all this, she thought for a moment, and said,

"If those old people next-door hadn't mattered so much to me, I wouldn't have gone to such lengths to find a *solution*, and none of this would have ever happened."

真正的音乐宇航员，远远超出了她最初那个想要在乐队里敲鼓的志向。

几年过后，当被问起她是如何达到这一成就的，她想了一会，说：

"如果隔壁的老人对我来说并不重要，我就不会想方设法去寻找解决办法，这一切也就不会发生了。"

solution *n.* 解决办法；处理手段

25

The Opera Singer

One day, a train was approaching the small town of Cheekyville. On the train was a strange guy with a big *suitcase*. He was called William Warbler—the man, not the suitcase—and he looked very common indeed. What made him most unusual, though, was the fact that whenever he needed to communicate he

歌剧演唱家

一天，一列火车正向小镇奇科维尔驶来。车上有个奇怪的人，带着一个大旅行箱。他叫歌手威廉——我说的是这个人的名字，不是旅行箱——他实际上看起来非常普通。可是他的不同之处在于，每当他需要交流时，他都会通过唱歌剧的方式。对威廉来说，哪怕是别人简单的一个问候，例如"日安"，他都会唱着来回答。他会清清嗓子这样回

---

suitcase *n.* 旅行箱

did it by singing opera. It didn't matter to William whether it was simply a matter of answering a brief greeting, like "good day". He would clear his voice and respond,

"Gooood dayyy to youuuuuuuu..... tooOOOO!"

It wouldn't be unfair to say that almost everyone considered William Warbler a massive pain in the neck. No one could get a normal, spoken word out of him. And, as no one knew how he made his living—and he lived quite simply, always wearing his same old second-hand suit—they often treated him with *disdain*.

They made fun of his singing, calling him "Don No One", "Poor-Rotti", and "Lazy Miserables". William had been in Cheekyville for some years, when, one day, a *rumour* spread round town like wildfire: William had secured a role in a very important opera in the nation's capital, and there were posters everywhere advertising the event. Everyone in the capital went to see it, and it was a great

---

复：

　　"你……也……日……安！"

　　可以这么说，几乎所有人都认为威廉很讨厌。没人能从他嘴里听到一个正常的、说出来的词。也没人知道他以什么为生，大家总是鄙视他。他生活非常简朴，总是穿着同一件别人穿过的旧套装。

　　他们嘲笑他唱的歌，叫他"无名氏先生"，"可怜的罗蒂"，以及"悲惨懒汉"。威廉已经在奇科维尔待了有些年了，一天，传闻像野火一样在小镇蔓延开来，听说威廉在都城一个很重要的歌剧里获得了一个角色，到处都张贴着关于这件事的宣传海报。都城里所有人都去看了，演出非常成功。演

---

disdain　*n.*　鄙视；蔑视　　　　　　　　　　　　rumour　*n.*　传闻

success. At the end of its run—to everyone in Cheekyville's surprise— when William was being interviewed by reporters, he answered their questions by speaking rather than singing. And he did it with great *courtesy* , and with a clear and pleasant voice.

From that day, William gave up singing at all hours. Now he did it only during his stage appearances and world tours. Some people *suspected* why he had changed, but others still had no idea, and continued believing him to be somewhat mad. They wouldn't have thought so if they had seen what William kept in his big suitcase. It was a large stone, with a hand-carved message on it.

The message said: "Practice, my boy. Practice every second, for you never know when your chance will come."

Little did people realise that he only got the role in the opera because the director had heard William singing while out buying a newspaper.

出结束时——出乎所有人意料的是——当威廉接受记者采访时，他回答他们的问题是用说的，而不是唱。而且，他的用语很有礼貌，嗓音通透悦耳。

那天以后，威廉不再像以前那样时时刻刻都在唱了。现在他只在舞台上和世界巡演中才唱。有人会猜测他为什么变了，但是其他人仍然没什么别的想法，依然继续相信他有些疯疯癫癫的。如果他们看到威廉那个大旅行箱里装的是什么就不会再那么想了。里面是块大石头，石头上是手工雕刻的字。

上面说的是："练习吧，我的孩子。抓住每一秒练习，因为你永远不会料到机会什么时候会来临。"

几乎没人知道，威廉之所以得到歌剧中的那个角色，是因为导演在外面买报纸的时候听到了他的歌声。

---

courtesy *n.* 礼貌   suspect *v.* 怀疑

26

Chess of a Thousand Colours

Brian Bristles was an *artistic* kind of a boy. He looked at everything as though it were a beautiful painting, and, in the blink of an eye, he could paint anything at all, filling it with magic and colour.

One day, Brian and his grandfather went to spend a weekend at the palace of the *Marquis* of Castling. The Marquis was

---

五颜六色的象棋

布莱恩·布瑞斯通是个很有艺术才华的男孩。他把每样东西都看成是一幅漂亮的绘画作品，而且他能在一瞬间就画出任何事物，画得色彩缤纷、惟妙惟肖。

一天，布莱恩和他的爷爷去卡瑟林侯爵的宫殿过周末。侯爵是布莱恩爷爷的老朋友，也是一位非常有名的象棋棋手。当他们来到宫殿以后，布莱恩

---

artistic *adj.* 有艺术天赋的；有美术才能的   marquis *n.* 侯爵

an old friend of Brian's grandfather; and was a very famous chess player. When they arrived, Brian went into a large room and found a lovely chess set, totally hand carved, and with its own *marble* table which acted as the board. This chess set caught Brian's artistic eye. However, he felt that these pieces were too *uniform*. Along with the blacks and whites of the board, it *amounted* to rather a *bland* set.

So, that night, paint box in hand, he tiptoed from his room to the chess room. There he spent the night painting each piece in the most colourful way. When the pieces were done, he painted a beautiful scene on the marble chessboard. Brian hoped to use his art to really surprise his grandfather and the Marquis.

However, the next morning, when the Marquis discovered that his pieces had been covered in a thousand colours, instead of being pleased, he was very angry. That afternoon he had a very important

---

走进一个很大的房间，发现一副非常可爱的象棋，完全是手工雕刻的，还有专门的大理石桌子作为棋盘。这副象棋吸引了具有艺术眼光的布莱恩。可是他觉得那些棋子太千篇一律了，加上棋盘上的白底黑格，就是一副平淡无奇的象棋。

于是，那天晚上布莱恩拿着颜料盒，蹑手蹑脚地从自己的房间走去象棋室。他花了一夜给所有棋子涂上五彩缤纷的颜色，之后又在大理石棋盘上画了一幅美丽的风景。布莱恩希望用他的绘画艺术给他的爷爷以及侯爵带来惊喜。

然而，第二天早上，当侯爵发现他的棋子被画得五颜六色时，他不但不

---

marble *n.* 大理石　　　　　　　uniform *adj.* 统一的；一律的
amount *v.* 相当于；等于　　　　bland *adj.* 乏味的；平淡无奇的

match to play. However lovely all those colours were, it would be impossible to play chess without being able to know which pieces were which; and even more difficult now that the squares of the board were covered with a painting.

Brian's grandfather explained to him that even the loveliest, most colourful things need some sense of order to them. The boy felt very hurt, remembering how many times his paintings had annoyed people...

But Brian Bristles was a true artist, and he wasn't about to give up easily. A little while later he went to his grandfather and the Marquis, and asked their *permission* to *rectify* what he had done to the chess set. Knowing how *ingeniously* artistic the boy was, they decided to give him a chance, so Brian went off and spent hours alone with his paints.

高兴，反而非常生气。那天下午他有一场非常重要的象棋比赛。不管这些五颜六色的棋子有多么可爱，如果分不清哪个棋子是什么，就无法下棋。而现在连棋盘上的格子也被绘画给遮住了，就更下不了棋了。

布莱恩的爷爷向布莱恩解释道，即便是最可爱、最多彩的东西也要有条理。想起他的绘画经常惹恼别人，布莱恩很伤心……

可是布莱恩·布瑞斯通是个真正的艺术家，他不会轻易地放弃。过了一会儿，他去找他的爷爷和侯爵，请他们允许他改正在那副象棋上所犯的错误。他们知道布莱恩是个很有艺术天分的孩子，所以决定再给他一次机会。于是布莱恩走了，一个人在象棋室里待了好几个小时。

---

permission *n.* 许可；允许　　　　　　　　rectify *v.* 改正；纠正
ingeniously *adv.* 心灵手巧地；机敏地

When he was finished, shortly before the match was about to begin, he called for the two men and showed them his work. What a beautiful chess set it now was!

Now there were two perfectly *recognisable* teams; that of night and that of day. On one side, the board and the pieces had been *decorated* with dozens of stars and moons of all sizes and colours. On the other side the decorations were suns, clouds, and rainbows. It was done so well that the whole set had an *unmatchable* sense of order and harmony.

Brian understood that a little order had been missing, but he had now managed to *impose* some without giving up any colour. The two grown-ups looked at the paintings and smiled. It was obvious that Brian Bristles would become a great artist.

在象棋比赛开始前不久，布莱恩完成了，他叫来爷爷和侯爵，向他们展示他的作品。现在这副象棋真是漂亮极了！

现在，两边的棋盘和棋子非常好区分，一边是黑夜，一边是白天。在黑夜的一边，棋盘和棋子上面画着不同颜色、不同大小的星星和月亮。在白天的一边，棋盘和棋子上面画着太阳、云彩和彩虹。画得太漂亮了，整副棋看上去既有条理又很和谐。

布莱恩明白了，原来的那副棋缺失了一点秩序，但是现在，他没有减少颜色，却增添了秩序。他的爷爷和侯爵看看他的绘画，笑了。显然，布莱恩·布瑞斯通会成为一位伟大的艺术家。

---

recognisable *adj.* 可认出的
unmatchable *adj.* 无可比拟的

decorate *v.* 装饰
impose *v.* 把……强加于

27

The Magic Key

Martin was now so old that for his birthday that year his father gave him a book without any pictures in it! Martin's father noticed his *disappointment*, and told him, "Son, this isn't just any old book, it's a magic book. But to discover its magic you'll have to read it."

魔法钥匙

马丁已经长大了，所以他爸爸给他买了一本不带图画的书作为他那年的生日礼物。他爸爸注意到他很失望，所以对他说："儿子，这本书跟以前的书不同，它是一本有魔力的书。不过，要想发现它的魔力，你得自己看这本书。"

disappointment *n.* 失望

Well, that was better; Martin liked everything to do with magic. He started reading it, even though he wasn't *overly enthusiastic*. The next morning, his father asked him, "Have you found the magic key?"

So... there was a key to find! Martin ran off and *flicked* through the book, but there was no sign of the key. He came back, very annoyed, but his father warned him, "You won't find it like that. You have to read the book."

Martin didn't have much patience, and he stopped reading the book, thinking his father was trying to trick him into reading a bit more, just as Martin's teacher had suggested to his dad. A little later, his sister, Angela, who was just a bit younger than him, asked him for the book so she could try reading it. After several days of trying to read it without great success, she appeared in the *lounge*, happily

---

　　他爸爸这么说还好点儿，马丁喜欢一切与魔法有关的东西。他开始看书了，虽然不是十分感兴趣。第二天早晨，他爸爸问他："你找到魔法钥匙了吗？"

　　这么说书里面有一把钥匙！马丁跑回房间，快速地翻阅那本书，可是根本没有发现钥匙的影子。他非常气愤地回来了，但是他爸爸提醒他："你这样是找不到钥匙的。你得认真地阅读那本书。"

　　马丁没什么耐心，不再看那本书了，认为他爸爸只是想办法骗他多看一点儿而已，就像他的老师向他爸爸提的建议一样。过了一会儿，马丁的妹妹安吉拉管马丁要那本书，她想看看。过了几天，安吉拉还没有看多少，她在起居室里高兴地尖叫："我找到了！我找到魔法书里的钥匙了！"她不停地

---

overly *adv.* 很；十分
flick *v.* 快速翻阅；浏览

enthusiastic *adj.* 热情的；热烈的
lounge *n.* 起居室

screaming, "I've found it! I've found the key of the magic book!" And she would not stop talking about all the worlds and places she had visited using that magic key.

All the talk ended up convincing Martin to *resume* reading the book. At first it was a pain; there wasn't even one *miserable* picture in the thing. But, gradually, the story started *springing* to life, and Martin got interested in the *adventurous* Prince's life. Then, suddenly, he was there.

The book itself was the key!

It was true that whenever he opened it, he felt transported to its valleys and seas, and he lived the adventures of its pirates, Princes, and wizards, as though they were himself. And his head and his dreams filled with adventures whenever they got a chance.

讲述着她用那把魔法钥匙去过的各个世界和地方。

听完安吉拉说的这些话，马丁继续去看那本书。开始的时候很痛苦，书里甚至连一张叫人讨厌的图片也没有。但是渐渐地，故事开始有了活力，马丁对王子的冒险生活产生了兴趣。后来他突然感觉自己就是王子。

原来那本书本身就是魔法钥匙！

后来，不管马丁什么时候翻开那本书，他都感觉自己仿佛置身于书中描述的山谷和海洋，亲身体验了海盗、王子和巫师们的冒险经历。他的脑海和梦里都充满了冒险和奇遇。

---

resume *v.* 重新开始；继续
spring *v.* 突然出现

miserable *adj.* 令人不快的；使难受的
adventurous *adj.* 爱冒险的；惊险的

However, the best thing about that story was that *from then on*, in every new book, he saw a new key to a thousand worlds and adventures. Martin never stopped travelling and travelling on those letters and words.

　　然而，这个故事最大的作用是，从此在每本新书里，马丁都看到了一把新的通往一千个世界和冒险的钥匙。他从来没有停止在字母和词汇的海洋里畅游。

---

from then on　从那时起

28

Colourful Animals

Along, long time ago each kind of animal lived in their own *special* land that was the same colour as themselves. It had always been this way, and no animal knew any different.

丰富多彩的动物

很久很久以前，每种动物都住在他们自己专门的一块土地上，土地的颜色就跟他们本身的颜色一样。因为一直都是这样，所以动物们都不知道还有其他不同的土地和颜色。

special *adj.* 特有的；特别的

One day, in the land of the orange elephants, a little bird swore that he had seen some *purple* cows. No one believed him, so the bird asked them to follow him to the *border*. When they arrived, they could see that it was true. Off in the distance was a completely purple land. The purple cows were equally amazed to see orange elephants. The two groups of animals got together and decided to go in search of the land of the dark blue *crocodiles* .

And so began a journey through many lands of many colours, each adding its own special animal to the *expedition* . When all the animals were together, heavy rain began pouring, and the rain mixed the animals' colours up, leaving each one with the colour they have today.

　　一天，在橙色大象的土地上，一只小鸟发誓，说他见过紫色的奶牛。可是没人相信他，所以这只小鸟让他们跟他一起去边境。当他们到达边境以后，发现小鸟说的是事实。远处是一片纯紫色的土地。紫色的奶牛看到橙色的大象也很吃惊。这两群动物聚在一起，决定去寻找深蓝色鳄鱼的土地。

　　于是动物们开始了一次旅程，穿越了许多不同颜色的土地。每经过一片土地，都会有新的动物加入这次征程。当所有动物都聚在一起时，天空开始下起了倾盆大雨。雨水把动物们的颜色都混在了一起，让他们变成了今天的颜色。

---

purple *adj.* 紫色的
crocodile *n.* 鳄鱼

border *n.* 边界；边境
expedition *n.* 远征队；探险队

29

The Cloudsqueezer

Wincey Wise was a young lady who worked cleaning the King's advisers' building. She was a very intelligent and *studious* girl, and wasn't

云朵挤压器

文茜·怀斯是个年轻女孩，她的工作是给国王的顾问们打扫房子。她很聪明也很好学，不会浪费在这些智者身边学习的机会。虽然如此，在透过钥匙孔听顾问们开会一年以后，她很担心，因为这

---

studious *adj.* 好学的；勤奋的

going to waste the opportunity of being around these wise men. Even so, after a year there, listening to their meetings through the *keyhole*, she was worried. The wise men never talked about anything new. They just went on about old matters: when he did this and he learned that.

Wincey had been reading all the books the men mentioned, and about all the subjects they discussed. But there came a time when she didn't know what to learn next. She had read everything on what the advisers talked about. So Wincey started reading about all kinds of other things.

Meanwhile, a very long *drought* had begun — something which had never happened in that land. The wise men *proposed* solutions, but as it was something that had never happened before, none of their ideas worked. Wincey, who had read all about climate, and seeing that she knew a great deal more than them, dared to interrupt

---

些智者从来不讨论新内容，只是不断地谈论旧话题，诸如他干了什么、他学了什么之类。

文茜阅读了顾问们提到的所有书籍，学习了他们讨论过的所有话题。但是在这之后，她不知道接下来要学什么了。她已经把顾问们谈论的一切都学会了，所以她开始看其他各个方面的书。

同时，当地发生了长期干旱，而当地此前从没发生过干旱。顾问们提出各种解决办法，但因为此前从未发生过干旱，所以他们的办法都没有用。文茜看过气候方面的全部图书，发现自己比顾问们懂得要多得多，于是大胆地打断了他们的商议，想提出一些解决办法。顾问们完全不理她，说她只不过

---

keyhole *n.* 锁眼；钥匙孔　　　　　　　　　　drought *n.* 干旱
propose *v.* 提议

their *deliberations* to suggest some solutions. The advisers ignored her; they said she was just a girl, that they were the experts, and not to bother them again.

Wincey felt so saddened and offended that she gave up her job there, went home, and spent several days holed up in her attic. When she left she was pushing a *trolley*, and she pushed it straight to the palace. She showed the King her invention: a strange *contraption* with lots of buttons and a huge *tuba* sticking out the top.

"This is the Cloudsqueezer," said Wincey. "It will put an end to the drought."

"Hmm," said the King, looking doubtful, "does it really work?"

Wincey bent over the machine, whispered a few words into it, and the words were transformed into strange deep noises, which came out of the tuba, like a speaker. Soon, a light shower began falling outside. It stopped as suddenly as it had started.

是个小姑娘而已，而他们才是专家，叫她不要再打扰他们。

文茜既难过又很生气，于是辞去工作回家了。她在阁楼里待了好几天。当她从阁楼出来时，她推着一辆手推车，一直推到皇宫。她向国王展示了她的发明——一个很奇怪的装置，上面带有很多按钮，顶端还伸出一个大喇叭。

"这是云朵挤压器"，文茜说道。"它能结束干旱。"

"嗯，"国王很怀疑地说，"它真的有用吗？"

文茜弯腰对机器说了几句悄悄话，这些话被转换成奇怪的深沉的响声。响声从大喇叭传出来，这个大喇叭就像个扬声器一样。不一会儿，外面突然下起了阵雨，然后又突然停了。

---

deliberation *n.* 仔细考虑；商议
contraption *n.* 装置

trolley *n.* 手推车
tuba *n.* 大号

"Did you cast a spell?" said the King. "Are you some kind of witch?"

"You what?" answered Wincey. "It's just a bit of science."

The King seemed to approve, and he called for his advisers to come and see the new invention. Wincey gave another *demonstration* . On seeing the rain fall, the advisers launched into a great *scholarly* debate. Was the effect based on *atmospheric turbulence* ? Was it a product of lunar reflectivity? And so many other equally ignorant theories that Wincey couldn't help but chuckle to herself.

While they had been theorising, the rain outside just got harder and harder. It ended up raining heavier than anyone had ever seen. The advisers kept talking, and it rained all the harder. So much so, that the King had to tell Wincey to disconnect the machine. She turned off the Cloudsqueezer, and the rain stopped. In front of astonished faces, she explained,

---

"你念咒语了吗？"国王说道。"你是巫师吗？"

"什么？"文茜答道。"这只是一点简单的科学知识而已。"

国王好像表示赞同，他把他的顾问们叫过来看看这个新发明。文茜又演示了一次。顾问们在看到下雨之后展开了一场激烈的学术讨论。这是大气湍流的作用吗？还是月亮反射的结果？顾问们想出了很多无知的理论，文茜忍不住偷着乐起来。

当他们还在推理的时候，外面的雨越下越大，最后下到前所未有的大。顾问们还在说着，雨继续越下越大。最后国王不得不让文茜关掉机器。她把云朵挤压器关掉以后雨就停了。她向这些惊讶的人们解释道：

---

demonstration *n.* 示范   scholarly *adj.* 学术性的
atmospheric *adj.* 大气的   turbulence *n.* 湍流；涡流

"The Cloudsqueezer is just a translator. It translates and amplifies words so that the clouds can understand them."

"So, how come it starts to rain?" asked the King.

"Ahh, that's because the clouds have a good sense of humour. Every time they hear a bit of foolishness they cry with laughter!"

Everyone looked *accusingly* at the King's advisers, and the wise men could do nothing but blush like tomatoes, in shame. That experience turned out of great use to the King. Not only did the drought come to an end, but, from that day on, they always kept the Cloudsqueezer switched on. To avoid being shamed by the clouds tears of laughter, the people of that land soon learned to study what they could, and to keep quiet on themes about which they were ignorant.

"云朵挤压器只不过是一台翻译机，它把听到的话翻译过来并把声音放大，这样云朵就能理解了。"

"那么，它是怎么开始下雨的呢？"国王问道。

"啊，那是因为云朵很有幽默感。他们一听到傻话，就会笑出眼泪来！"

所有人都责备地看着国王的顾问们。这些智者什么也做不了，只是羞愧得满脸通红。这次经历对国王很有用处。不仅干旱停止了，而且从那天开始，他们总是开着云朵挤压器。因为不想被云朵嘲笑而丢脸，当地的人们很快就开始尽量多学习知识，对于他们不知道的话题就会保持沉默。

---

accusingly *adv.* 谴责地；指责地

30

The Homework Party

"Charlieeeeeeee, do your homework now!" Wow, his mother was really *bellowing* at him.

Charlie thought, "Well, she doesn't have to do it. It's so boring," and he spent hours with his books, hoping that time would pass and it would soon be time for supper. As usual, he was lying on his bed, busy

---

家庭作业聚会

"查理！快做作业！"哇，查理的妈妈冲他大喊。

查理心想："她倒是不用做作业。烦死了。"他看了几个小时的书，希望时间快点儿过去，很快就到吃晚饭的时间。他像往常一

---

bellow *v.* 大声吼叫

staring at the ceiling, *daydreaming*. Suddenly some little elves , no more than a *centimetre* tall, appeared by the window.

"Good evening, young man, will you please give us your homework so we can play with it?" asked one of the elves, politely.

Charlie laughed.

"How are you lot going to play with homework? It's the most boring stuff there is! Ha, ha, ha... Go on, take it. You can play with it as long as you like".

Charlie watched his guests, and was so surprised to see what they did. In less than a minute, they had formed teams and were busy playing with the pen, the eraser, the book, and the pad of paper. Very strange stuff they were getting up to. Like with the *sums*, instead of moving the pen across the paper, they would hold the pen still and move the paper instead. Or like how they had races to

---

样，躺在床上盯着天花板，做着白日梦。突然窗边出现了几个不足一厘米高的小精灵。

"晚上好，年轻人，能把你的作业给我们玩玩吗？"其中一个小精灵礼貌地问道。

查理大笑。

"你们要怎么玩我的作业呢？它是世上最无聊的东西了！哈哈哈……给，拿去吧。只要你们喜欢，想怎么玩就怎么玩。"

查理看着他的客人们，看到他们的所作所为他感到很惊讶。在不到一分钟的时间里，他们分成小组，摆弄着笔、橡皮、书本和一叠纸。他们做的事

---

daydream *v.* 做白日梦　　　　　　　　　　　centimetre *n.* 厘米
sum *n.* 计算；算数

see who could do the sums fastest. And then they all dressed up as either Father Christmas, a *Halloween pumpkin*, or a bag of cheese. And whenever the clock was stopped, the *elf* who was in the lead got to draw himself in the *notepad* .

So the pad ended up full of Santas and pumpkins. They were also really funny while learning to read. They used well-known songs, and had to learn the words to them. When they had done that they put on a big concert to sing those songs.

Charlie really enjoyed watching those little students, he even joined in with the singing. And time passed so quickly, that suddenly his mother was calling him for supper.

都很奇怪。比如算数的时候，他们不是拿笔在纸上写，而是手握着笔不动，却移动纸。他们还比赛看谁计算得最快。他们都打扮成圣诞老人、万圣节南瓜，或者一袋奶酪的模样。每当计时停止的时候，最先算完的小精灵会在记事本里画一幅自己的画。

最后记事本里画满了圣诞老人和南瓜。学习朗读的时候他们也很有趣。他们利用著名的歌曲，跟着歌曲的旋律朗读。当他们学会以后，就会开一场盛大的音乐会来演唱那些歌曲。

查理非常喜欢看着这些小学生们，他甚至加入他们，跟他们一起唱。时间过得很快，他妈妈突然叫他吃晚饭了。

Halloween *n.* 万圣节前夜   pumpkin *n.* 南瓜
elf *n.* 小精灵；小妖精   notepad *n.* 记事本；笔记本

"Aww, what a pain! This is so much fun..." he *groaned* , as he got up to go to supper.

"Of course it's fun! I already told you. Why don't you try it for a few days yourself? We'll all come back to see you again from time to time."

"Deal!" agreed Charlie.

So, every evening, Charlie started playing with his homework, inventing new and crazier ways to make it more fun. He would dress up, sing loads of songs, and do all manner of other things too. Now and again, his elf friends would turn up, although the truth was that he wasn't sure whether they really had come through the window or from out of his own imagination.

Neither Charlie's parents, nor his teachers, nor anyone in the

"啊，太遗憾了！这太有意思了……"他起身去吃饭时抱怨道。

"当然有意思了！我告诉过你的。你何不自己尝试几天呢？我们都会时不时地回来看你的。"

"好吧，就这么办！"查理答应了。

于是，每天晚上查理都开始跟他的家庭作业一起玩，发明新的疯狂的方式来使做作业更有趣。他打扮自己、唱很多歌，做各种不同的事。他的小精灵朋友们会时不时地出现，虽然他也不知道他们是通过窗户进来的，还是他自己想象出来的。

查理的父母、老师和学校里的所有人都不明白查理怎么会发生如此巨大

groan *v.* 不高兴地低声说；咕哝

whole school could understand the great change in him. From that day on, not only did he spend a lot more time doing homework, he did it perfectly, and *accompanied* with lots of drawings. He was very happy, and was always singing. His mother told him how proud she was at seeing him work so hard, especially at something she knew he found boring.

But Charlie said to himself, "Well, she doesn't have to do it. It's fun!"

的变化。从那天起,查理不仅花很多时间做作业,而且做得非常好,还画了很多画。他非常开心,总是哼着歌。他的妈妈告诉他,看到他本来觉得学习很无聊,可是他现在如此用功地学习,她感到十分骄傲。

可是查理自言自语道: "唉,可惜她不用做作业。这很有意思!"

accompany *v.* 伴随

31

The Math Dunce

That year, in the local school, there was a new Math teacher, as well as some new pupils. One of the new kids was the stupidest child anyone had ever seen. It made no difference how quickly or how slowly they tried explaining numbers to him; he would always end up saying something *enormously dumb* . Like two plus

数学笨蛋

那一年，当地的学校来了一位新数学老师，还有几个新学生。其中一个新生是所有人见过的最笨的孩子。不管大家向他解释数字时有多快或有多慢，他都学不会。他总是会说一些极其愚蠢的话。比如，二加二等于五，七乘以三等于二十七，或者一个三角形有三十个

---

enormously *adv.* （范围、程度）极大地　　　　dumb *adj.* 愚蠢的

two was five, seven times three was twenty-seven, or a *triangle* had thirty corners...

Before this boy arrived, Maths lessons had been the most boring of all. Now they were great fun. Encouraged by the new teacher, the children would listen to the pieces of *nonsense spouted* by the new kid, and they would have to correct his mistakes.

They all wanted to be the first to find his mistakes, and then think up the most *original* ways to explain them. To do this they used all kinds of stuff: sweets, playing cards, oranges, paper planes...

It didn't seem like any of this bothered the new kid. However, little Lewis was sure that it was bound to make him feel sad inside. So, one day, he decided to follow the new kid home after school; Lewis was sure he would see him crying.

角……

　　在这个男孩来以前，数学课是最无聊的课，现在却变得非常有趣了。在新老师的鼓励下，孩子们要听这个新生不停地胡说，还得纠正他的错误。

　　他们都想做第一个发现他的错误的人，然后还要想出最有创意的方式来解释这些错误，因此他们用了各种各样的东西：糖果、玩牌、橘子、纸飞机……

　　这一切好像并没有困扰新来的孩子。然而，小路易斯相信，他心里一定很难过。所以一天，他决定放学后跟踪这个新生回家。路易斯相信他一定会看到他哭。

---

triangle *n.* 三角形
spout *v.* 滔滔不绝地说

nonsense *n.* 胡言乱语，胡扯
original *adj.* 有独创性的

On leaving school, the new kid walked a few minutes to a local park, and there he waited for a while, until someone came along to meet him...

It was the new teacher!

The teacher gave the new kid a hug, and off they went, hand in hand. Following from a *distance*, Lewis could hear they were talking about Math.

And that stupid new kid knew everything about it, much more than anyone in the class!

离开学校以后，这个新生走了几分钟，来到当地的一个公园。他在那儿等了一会儿，直到有人来接他……

是新来的老师！

老师给新生一个拥抱，然后他们手拉手一起走了。路易斯远远地跟着，他听到他们在谈论数学。

这个愚蠢的新生什么都知道，比班级里的任何人知道的都多！

---

distance *n.* 距离；间距

32

The Gossips

Sarah and Mark were a pair of champion *gossips*. They were always spying, and poking their noses into anything and everything. And how they loved to broadcast what they had discovered—which was a lot, and very little of it good. People had often explained to them the importance of respecting others' *privacy*, but they would just reply, "If they

爱嚼舌根的人

萨拉和马克最爱说别人闲话了。他们总是窥探、干涉所有事情。他们非常喜欢宣扬他们发现的好多事——基本上没有什么好事情。别人总是解释给他们听,告诉他们尊重他人隐私的重要性,可是他们只是答道:"如果他们没有什么要隐瞒的就不会在意了。我们没有任何需

---

gossip n. 爱说长道短的人   privacy n. 隐私;私事

had nothing to hide then they wouldn't mind. We have nothing to hide, so we couldn't care less."

Then, one day, a poor, bad-tempered wizard with very few powers, crossed their path. Sarah and Mark managed to break one of the wizard's tricks, so the wizard decided to get his revenge by using a strange spell which would give all the children a good laugh, before he moved on. The next day, when Sarah and Mark were sitting in class, the emergency speaker came on. It was the wizard's voice. He said,

"Ding dong dinnnng! Ding dong dinnnng! Attention! Sarah Jones thinks Robert is very good-looking, and she'd like to be his girlfriend. Ding dong dinnnng!"

How embarrassed Sarah felt! She hadn't told anyone how she felt about Robert, and she turned as red as a *ripe* tomato. There was

要隐瞒的，所以，我们一点都不在乎。"

然后，有一天，一个可怜的坏脾气巫师碰到了他俩。萨拉和马克识破了巫师的一个把戏，所以巫师决定要在离开之前报复，他施了一个奇怪的咒语，这咒语会让所有的孩子们大笑一场的。第二天，当萨拉和马克正在上课时，紧急喇叭里传出了巫师的声音。他说：

"叮咚叮！叮咚叮！注意了！萨拉·琼斯觉得罗伯特非常英俊，她想当他的女朋友。叮咚叮！"

萨拉真是太尴尬了！她没告诉过任何人她对罗伯特的想法，她的脸红得像熟透了的西红柿。课堂上一阵骚动，直到喇叭再次响起，喧闹声才稍稍平

ripe *adj.* （水果、谷物等）成熟的

quite a *commotion* in class, and the noise only subsided when the speaker came on again:

"Attention! Right now, Mark Smith is thinking that Anthony Wilson is a fat and rather foolish *gorilla*, and that if he—Smith—were a bit bigger, he'd give Wilson a seriously good beating. Ding dong dinnnng!"

Mark dearly wanted to run out of the classroom to hide.

And so it went. Throughout the day the speaker would come on and reveal the *innermost* thoughts of our two little gossips. With every passing minute their trouble and embarrassment were mounting. So much so, that eventually the two of them went over to the speaker, crying with anger, and demanding that the voice stop reporting their thoughts.

"If you have nothing to hide then it shouldn't bother you," answered the wizard.

息：

"注意了！现在，马克·史密斯正在想安东尼·威尔逊是只又肥又蠢的大猩猩，如果他——史密斯——再壮一点的话，他会把威尔逊一顿好打。叮咚叮！"

马克真想要跑出教室躲起来。

就这样，喇叭一整天都在不断地揭露这两个爱搬弄是非的小家伙内心深处的想法。每过一分钟他们的麻烦和尴尬就增加一分。直到最后他们俩走到喇叭前，气得哭了起来，要求喇叭不要再揭发他们的想法了。

"如果你们没有什么要隐瞒的就没什么烦心的，"巫师回答道。

---

commotion *n.* 骚动　　　　　　　　　　　　　　　gorilla *n.* 大猩猩
innermost *adj.* 内心深处的

"Of course we have nothing to hide!" they answered, "but those are private thoughts!" And their complaints continued.

After a while the complaints *petered* out, and Sarah and Mark looked at each other. They had finally realised that what the wizard was now doing was exactly what they themselves had been doing all their lives. After they promised not to gossip any more about other people's private lives, the wizard removed the spell and said goodbye to them all.

And every child in that class long remembered that *hilarious* morning at school, where they were given a most effective lesson on the importance of respecting others' privacy.

"我们当然没什么可隐瞒的！"他们答道，"但是那些是私人想法！"他们继续抱怨着。

过了一会，他们的抱怨声渐渐消失了，萨拉和马克互相看着。他们终于意识到巫师正在做的事情正是他们自己一直在做的。他们承诺，再也不说长道短、评论他人的私生活了，这之后，巫师去除了咒语，和大家说再见离开了。

课堂上的所有孩子很长时间都记得在学校的那个极其滑稽的早上，那个早上，他们上了很生动的一课，学到了尊重他人隐私是多么重要。

---

peter *v.* 慢慢消失　　　　　　hilarious *adj.* 极其滑稽的

33

Colourless Tiger

Once upon a time, there was a *colourless* tiger. All his shades were greys, blacks and whites. So much so, that he seemed like something out of an old black and white movie. His lack of colour had made him so famous that the world's greatest painters had come to his zoo to try to put some colour on him. None of them

丢了色彩的老虎

从前有一只没有色彩的老虎。他身上所有的颜色除了灰色、黑色，就是白色。这让他看起来像是从老旧的黑白电影里走出来的。他因为缺少色彩变得很有名，连世界上最伟大的画家们都来到他的动物园试图给他画上颜色。可是没有一个人成功过，颜色总是顺着他的毛皮

colourless *adj.* 无色的；苍白的

succeeded, as the colours would always just drip down off his skin.

Then along came Van Cough the crazy painter. He was a strange guy who travelled all about, happily painting with his brush. Well, it would be more accurate to say that he moved his brush about, as if to paint; because he never put any paint on his brush, and neither did he use *canvas* or paper. He painted the air, and that's why they called him Van Cough. So, when he said he wanted to paint the colourless tiger, everyone had a good laugh.

When entering the tiger's cage he began *whispering* in the animal's ear, and moving his dry brush up and down the tiger's body. And to everyone's surprise, the tiger's skin started to take on colour, and these were the most vivid colours any tiger had ever had. Van Cough spent a long time whispering to the animal, and making slight adjustments to his painting. The result was truly beautiful.

滴落下来。

　　然后，疯狂的画家梵卡来了。他是个奇怪的家伙，四处旅行，用他的刷子快乐地作画。唉，还是这样说更精确：他挥舞着他的刷子，就好像在画画一样；因为他的刷子从来不蘸颜料，他也从来不用画布或者画纸。他在空气里画画，所以人们才叫他"梵卡"（译者注：取画家"梵高"的谐音）。当他说他要给这只没有色彩的老虎画上颜色时，大家都不禁大笑。

　　进入老虎笼他就开始对着这只动物的耳朵小声低语着，在老虎身上上下挥舞着他的干刷子。让大家吃惊的是，老虎的皮肤开始呈现出颜色，这些颜色是所有老虎拥有过的最生动的色彩。梵卡和老虎耳语了好长时间，给他的画做了些微调。这幅画作真是太美了。

---

canvas *n.* 画布　　　　　　　　　　　　　　　whisper *v.* 低语

Everyone wanted to know what the painter's secret was. He explained to them that his brush was only good for painting real life, and that to do that he needed no colours. He had managed to paint the tiger using a phrase he kept whispering in its ear: "In just a few days you will be free again, you shall see."

And seeing how sad the tiger had been in his *captivity*, and how joyful the tiger now seemed at the prospect of freedom, the zoo authorities transported him to the forest and set him free, where never again would he lose his colour.

　　所有人都想知道这个画家的秘密。他对他们解释说，他的刷子只善于绘画生活，画生活是不需要颜料的。他之所以给老虎画上了色彩，是因为他不停地对着老虎的耳朵小声说着这样一句话："几天后你就会重新获得自由，你会看到的。"

　　看到老虎被关起来是多么伤心，看到他现在想到自由又是多么快乐，动物园的管理者便把他送到了森林里，叫他重获自由了，在那里，他将再也不会丢失他的色彩。

---

captivity *n.* 监禁；困住

34

The Respectful Prince and the Dwarves

Once upon a time, the King's two Princes were playing in a forest, and — meeting one at a time — they came across four dwarves who asked them to be more careful.

The first *dwarf* had a headache and he asked them not to shout. The second dwarf

---

恭敬的王子和小矮人们

从前，国王的两个王子在森林里玩，他们先后遇到了四个小矮人，他们请求他们玩的时候多留心一点。

第一个小矮人有头痛症，他请他们不要大喊。第二个小矮人正在画风景，要他们躲开点，因为他们挡住了光线。第三个小矮人正在路中央拼一个

---

dwarf *n.* 小矮人

QUALITY LIFE STORIES II

was painting a landscape, and he asked the children to move away because they were blocking out the light. The third dwarf was doing a giant *jigsaw* puzzle in the middle of the road, and he asked the children not to tread on it. The fourth dwarf was watching a butterfly and he asked them not to frighten it away.

The Prince who respected others did as the dwarves asked, but the disrespectful Prince ignored the dwarves' *pleas*, and kept bothering them. In the evening, both boys had become separated and lost. They needed to get back to the palace quickly.

Each of them separately came across the four dwarves again, and asked for their help. They refused to help the disrespectful Prince, but with the respectful Prince they did whatever they could to help,

---

很大的拼图，他请这两个孩子不要踩到图。第四个小矮人正在观赏一只蝴蝶，请求他们不要把蝴蝶吓跑。

那个尊重人的王子按照小矮人要求的做了，可是那个无礼的王子没有搭理小矮人们的请求，一直烦着他们。黄昏时候，两个孩子走散了，都迷了路。他们得快点回去才行。

他们俩分别再次遇到了这四个小矮人，并请求他们帮助。小矮人没有帮助那个无礼的王子，可是他们尽了最大努力去帮助那个尊敬他人的王子，带

---

jigsaw *n.* 拼图；拼板玩具

plea *n.* 请求

and took him along some secret *tracks* which led right to the palace.

The other Prince arrived much later, and was punished for it. He now understood that it's much better to respect everyone if you want to have friends.

他走了直接通向王宫的秘密小路。

　　另一个王子很晚才回去，因此受到了惩罚。他现在懂得了如果想要有朋友的话，你最好尊重每一个人。

track *n.* 小路

35

Jemima the Nosy Giraffe

In *Chipper* Jungle, everything was peaceful and happy until Jemima turned up. Jemima was an extremely tall *giraffe*, with a long bendy neck like some rubber plant. She got on everyone's nerves because she was just the *nosiest* and most gossipy animal anyone had ever known. What made it worse was that, thanks to her

---

爱管闲事的长颈鹿杰迈玛

快活林里一直是一派快乐祥和的景象，直到杰迈玛出现了。杰迈玛是个奇高无比的长颈鹿，有着灵活易弯的脖子，就像是橡胶树。她搅得所有人心神不宁，因为她是大家前所未见的最爱管闲事、最爱嚼舌头的动物。更糟糕的是，没有任何洞穴窝巢是她到不了的，这可多亏

---

chipper *adj.* 生气勃勃的   giraffe *n.* 长颈鹿
nosy *adj.* 爱管闲事的；爱打听的（也写作nosey）

height and her long, bendy neck, there was no den or nest beyond her reach. There she'd be, always sticking her head in.

She observed everything, and made sure everyone knew what was going on. This annoyed so many animals that they had a meeting and decided to teach her a lesson.

At that time Big Bongo, the most important of all the monkeys, decided to move to an old abandoned den, and he did the place up until it was the *cosiest* home in the whole jungle. Jemima couldn't help her curiosity, and one night she *tiptoed* over there and approached the bedroom window. The window was open and she stuck her head inside. She was just on time to see Big Bongo leaving the bedroom. So, Jemima pushed her neck further in so that she could follow him to the next room. It was dark inside and she couldn't see very well, but she followed him down a corridor, and

---

了她长得那么高，还有那么长那么灵活的脖子。她一到哪里就会把头伸进去。

她注意观察所有事情，并告知大家，让所有人都知道正在发生着什么。她这么做，惹恼了太多的动物，他们开会决定要给她上一课。

那时，猴子的首领大邦戈决定搬去一处遗弃的旧洞穴，他把那地方修缮一番，最后把它变成了整个丛林里最温暖舒服的家。杰迈玛又禁不住好奇了，一天晚上，她蹑手蹑脚地来到了大邦戈的家，靠到卧室的窗户。窗户开着，她把头伸了进去。正巧看到大邦戈离开卧室。于是，杰迈玛又伸了伸脖子，这样她就能跟着他去下一个房间了。里面非常黑，她几乎什么都看不清

---

cosy *adj.* 舒适温暖的   tiptoe *v.* 踮着脚走

then into another bedroom, and then another...

Until at last Jemima couldn't follow him any more. She had run out of neck. Big Bongo had ran all around his house, and now Jemima's neck was in one enormous tangle.

Then all the other animals, who were in on the trick, came over to the house to let Jemima know what they thought of her irritating *nosiness*. She felt so embarrassed that she decided from then on that she would use her long neck for more constructive tasks than poking into the lives of others.

楚，可是她跟着他来到了走廊，然后进到了另一个房间，又一个房间……

一直到杰迈玛再也不能跟着他了。她的脖子不够用了。大邦戈绕着他的房子跑了一圈，现在，杰迈玛的脖子打了一个巨大的结。

然后，所有参与其中的动物都来了，告诉杰迈玛，他们觉得她那么爱管闲事真的很讨厌。她感到非常尴尬，她决定以后会用她的长脖子做更有意义的事情，而不再打探别人的私生活了。

---

nosiness *n.* 爱管闲事

36

The Mysterious Juggling Clown

Once upon a time, a *juggling clown* came to a village. The clown went from town to town, earning a little money from his show. In that village he began his act in the square. While everyone was enjoying the show, a naughty boy started to make fun of the clown, telling him to leave the village. The shouts and insults made

神秘的杂耍小丑

从前，一个村子里来了一个杂耍小丑。小丑从一个小镇到另一个小镇，靠他的表演挣点微薄的收入。他在这个村子的广场上开始了表演。大家正在观看的时候，一个顽皮的男孩开始取笑起小丑，叫他离开村子。男孩的大喊和侮辱让小丑紧张不安起来，他掉了一个杂耍球。人群里其他人因为他的这个失误开始喝倒彩。最后，小丑只好赶快离开

juggle *v.* 玩杂耍　　　　　　　　　　　　　　　clown *n.* 小丑

the clown nervous, and he dropped one of his juggling balls. Some others in the crowd started *booing* because of this mistake, and in the end the clown had to leave quickly.

He ran off, leaving four of the juggling balls. But neither the clown nor his juggling balls were in any way ordinary. During that night, each one of the balls magically turned into a naughty boy, just like the one who had shouted the insults. All except one ball, which turned into another clown. For the whole of the next day, the copies of the naughty boy walked round the village, making trouble for everyone. In the afternoon, the copy of the clown started his juggling show, and the same thing happened as the previous day. But, this time, there were four naughty boys shouting, instead of one. Again, the clown had to run off, leaving another four balls behind.

3。

他跑开了，留下了四个杂耍球。不过，无论是这个小丑还是他的杂耍球，都一点不普通。那天晚上，这四个球里面有三个球神奇地变成了三个顽皮的男孩，就像那个大叫着侮辱人的男孩一样，另一个球变成了另一个小丑。第二天一整天，这几个杂耍球变成的顽皮的孩子们在村子里走了一圈，给所有人找麻烦。下午的时候，那个由球变成的小丑开始表演起了杂耍，前一天发生的事情再次发生了。但是，这次大声叫喊的男孩有四个，而不是一个。小丑不得不再次跑开了，留下了四个球。

---

boo *v.* 发嘘声；喝倒彩

Once more, during the night, three of those balls turned into copies of the naughty boy, and one turned into a clown. And so the same story repeated itself for several days, until the village was filled with naughty boys who would leave no one in peace. The village elders decided to put an end to all this. They made sure that none of the naughty boys would disrespect or insult anyone. When the clown's show began, the elders prevented the boys even making a *squeak* . So the clown managed to finish his show, and could spend that night in the village.

That night, three of the copies of the naughty boy disappeared, and the same happened until only the clown and the original naughty boy remained.

The boy, and everyone in the village, had been shown just how far

---

又一次，在这天晚上，三个球变成了顽皮的男孩，一个球变成了小丑。同样的事情就这样一直重复了好几天，最后，村子里满是顽皮的男孩，搅得所有人不得安宁。村里老人们决定要结束这一切。他们要确保所有这些顽皮的孩子不可以对任何人不敬。当小丑表演开始的时候，老人们阻止着他们的顽皮捣蛋，甚至连一声尖叫都不准他们发出来。所以，小丑顺利地完成了他的表演，当晚可以在村子里留宿了。

那天晚上，三个由球变成的男孩消失了，相同的情况一直发生着，直到最后只剩下这个小丑和村子里原来的那个顽皮的男孩。

男孩和村里的所有人都看到了他们可以做得多过火。从那以后，村里的

---

squeak *n.* 尖叫

they could go. From then on, instead of running visitors away, that village made every effort to make sure that visitors would spend a nice day there. The villagers had discovered just how much a *humble* travelling clown can teach with his show.

人不再赶走客人，而是尽最大努力确保客人们在那里度过愉快的一天。村民们发现，一个平凡的走街串巷的小丑用他的杂耍表演，让他们学到的太多了。

---

humble *adj.* *卑微的*

37

The Wicked Prince

There once was a King whose son was a dishonest *telltale* . This Prince would threaten to punish the servants if they ever let the King know this.

One day, the King and the Prince left the castle together. They arrived at a village, at which point they separated. The Prince went back to his normal behaviour, getting

邪恶的王子

从前有一个国王，他的儿子是个不诚实的告密者。王子威胁仆人，如果他们胆敢让国王知道这件事，就会惩罚他们。

一天，国王和王子一起出了城堡。他们到达一个村子之后就分开了。王子开始原形毕露，烦扰每一个人。可是国王没有事先通知就突然回来了，正

---

telltale *n.* 小告密者

on everyone's nerves, but the King returned *unannounced* and caught the Prince red-handed, up to his tricks.

The Prince took advantage of the fact that in that village there was a youth who looked just like him. He told his father that it had been the youth who had done all these bad things. However, the King, seeing what a lying *snitch* this person was, concluded that the boy in the village must be his real son, the Prince.

So the King took the boy back with him to the palace, and left the real Prince in the village. While there, the Prince finally came to *regret* his *previous* life filled with lies and accusations . The other young man heard of this, and decided to forgive the Prince. He confessed to the King that he wasn't his real son after all. The King left the castle and brought his son home, and the two young men ended up as inseparable friends.

好抓了王子一个正着，亲眼看见了他恶劣的行径。

村子里有个年轻人跟王子长得很像，而王子恰好利用了这一点。他跟国王说，所有这些坏事都是这个年轻人干的。然而，看到这个人既爱撒谎又爱告密，国王便认为村子里的年轻人一定才是他真正的儿子、真正的王子。

于是国王把村子里的男孩带回了宫殿，把真正的王子留在了村子里。在村子里，王子终于为他以前充满谎言和指责的生活感到后悔。宫殿里的年轻人听说了这一切之后，决定原谅王子。他向国王坦白自己不是他真正的儿子。于是国王出了城堡，把他的儿子带回了家，两个年轻人也成了形影不离的朋友。

---

unannounced *adj.* 未事先宣布的

regret *v.* 为……感到遗憾；后悔

snitch *n.* 告密者；告发者

previous *adj.* 早先的；先前的

38

Hammer Blows

aniel had a unique gift. He was the only person who could see everyone's "hammer of truth". At first he couldn't work out what that big *lump* of steel was, hanging over everyone's head. But, with time, he realised that it was connected to the little white lies people would say to avoid hurting or annoying

锤 击

丹尼尔有一项独特的天赋。他是唯一一个能够看见每个人的"真话之锤"的人。起初,他不明白悬挂在每个人头上的大铁块是什么。不过随着时间的流逝,他意识到,它和人们为了避免伤害或惹恼别

lump *n.* 一块

others.

Daniel saw that each time anyone told a person one of those little white lies, the hammer above the person's head would rise slightly. The more *deceived* someone was, the further above their head was the hammer. *Initially*, Daniel was amused to see some of the hammers hanging really high above, but then he discovered that the hammers always fall at some point. When the person discovered the truth, down it would fall.

"It's strange," he thought, seeing a hammer crash down onto an *unsuspecting* head, "everyone tries to keep this person from suffering, but all they're doing is... taking a run up to make sure the blow lands all the heavier!"

The discovery seemed so important to Daniel that he wrote a great book about the subject. Everyone told him how much they had enjoyed reading it, and what a good writer he was. He did *interviews*,

---

人而说的善意的谎言有关。

丹尼尔发现，每次有人向某人说一次善意的谎言时，被骗的人头上的锤子就会向上升起一点点。被欺骗得次数越多，锤子升得就越高。起初，丹尼尔看见有些锤子悬挂得非常高时感到很有趣，可是后来他发现，锤子总会在某个点降落。当这个人发现真相的时候，锤子就会落下来。

"太奇怪了，"看见锤子砸向毫无戒备之心的人的脑袋时，丹尼尔心想，"每个人都想防止这个人受到伤害，可是他们做的却是……让锤子击打得更重！"

丹尼尔觉得这个发现非常重要，所以他写了一本关于这个话题的书。每

---

deceive *v.* 欺骗
unsuspecting *adj.* 无疑心的；无戒心的

initially *adv.* 最初；开头
interview *n.* 采访

and began to give conferences. Daniel felt good about helping out so many people. That was, until one day someone asked him to sign a copy of his book. Daniel opened the book, and saw that it was empty... he only had time to quickly glance upwards before the great hammer blow fell.

No one had read the book. A printing error meant the book had been produced with no writing on the pages.

With all his dreams and *illusions* destroyed by that one hammer blow, Daniel sat and managed to smile. Without doubt, what he had needed was a book like his very own...

个人都告诉他他们很喜欢看这本书，而且他是个优秀的作家。他开始接受采访并召开讨论会。丹尼尔为帮到这么多的人而感到开心。直到有一天，有人请他在他的书上签名，丹尼尔打开书，看到里面是空的……他刚刚迅速向上瞥了一眼，大锤子就砸了下来。

根本没有人看过他的书。印刷错误导致这本书里根本就没有字。

丹尼尔所有的梦想和幻觉都被这一锤击摧毁了，他坐在那里，挤出微笑。毫无疑问，他需要一本像他自己这本一样的书……

---

illusion *n.* 幻觉；错觉

39

The Lie-hunting Wizard

The Great Wizard was a hunter of lies. He invented magic stones to help find the child who told most of them. The magic stones were beautiful, and with every lie they would grow bigger. The stones moved from person to person until they reached the worst of *liars*.

识破谎言的巫师

伟大的巫师是个谎言捕手。他发明了魔法石来帮助寻找撒谎最多的孩子。魔法石很漂亮，而且会随着谎言的增多而变大。魔石会从一个人手里跑到另一个人手里，一直到达最爱说谎的骗子的手里。

liar *n.* 说谎者

A little boy, who was a terrible liar, started collecting these magic stones, and when he had a great many of them, he decided to leave on a little boat.

When the boy and his boat were out at sea, the wizard appeared and started asking him questions about the stones. Because the boy only ever answered with lies, the stones started growing, and under their *weight* the boat began to sink.

The boy was frightened and started crying. He regretted telling so many lies, and he asked the wizard to *forgive* him. However, the wizard said that he would only save the boy if he would agree to become his *apprentice* .

The boy agreed, and spent many years as the wizard's *assistant* . Until one day the wizard retired , and the boy, who had been such a terrible liar, ended up being the new Great Wizard, hunter of lies.

　　一个非常爱撒谎的小男孩开始收集这些魔石。当他收集到很多的时候，他决定乘小船离开。

　　当男孩坐船出海以后，巫师出现了，开始问他关于魔石的问题。因为小男孩只用谎言来回答问题，所以魔石开始变大，在魔石的重压下小船开始下沉。

　　男孩很害怕，开始大哭。他很后悔说了那么多谎话，并请求巫师原谅他。然而巫师说，只有男孩同意做他的徒弟，他才会救男孩。

　　男孩同意了，他给巫师当了好多年的助手。直到有一天，巫师退休了，这个曾经非常爱撒谎的男孩成了新的伟大的巫师和谎言捕手。

---

weight *n.* 重量；分量　　　　　　　forgive *v.* 原谅；宽恕
apprentice *n.* 学徒；徒弟　　　　　　assistant *n.* 助手

40

The Hair Thief

Valerie was very worried about her daddy. For some time now she had noticed he was going *bald*. It seemed like every time she looked at him he had less hair than before. One day she rather *boldly* asked him, "Daddy, every day you have less hair. Why is that?"

偷头发的贼

瓦莱丽非常担心她的爸爸，因为她注意到他爸爸快要变成秃头了。好像她每看他一次，他的头发就会少一点儿。一天，她勇敢地问她爸爸："爸爸，你的头发一天比一天少。这是为什么呀？"

bald *adj.* 秃头的；光秃的   boldly *adv.* 大胆地；勇敢地

Her father smiled and said, "It's the hair thief. Round here there's a little *pilferer* , and he visits my head during the night when I'm asleep. One by one he pulls out my hairs, as many as he likes. And there's no way to catch him!"

This worried Valerie, but she was determined to help her daddy. That very night she stayed awake as long as she could. As soon as she heard the first *snuffles* of her father's *snoring* she grabbed a hammer and went straight to her parents' bedroom. She slowly tiptoed in, being careful not to make a sound. She didn't want the hair thief to hear her. When she arrived at her father's side she began *watchfully* inspecting his head, determined to catch the hair thief as soon as he appeared. Before long, she saw a shadow on her daddy's head and, with every last ounce of her strength, she swung the hammer down.

Thwack ! Her father let out an enormous yelp and in a single

她的爸爸笑着说：“是偷头发的贼干的好事。这附近有个小偷，夜里我睡觉的时候他就会来造访我的头。他把我的头发一根根地拔掉，想拔多少就拔多少。可是没有办法抓住他！”

这让瓦莱丽很担心，她决定帮助她的爸爸。那天晚上她坚持不睡觉。刚一听到她爸爸打呼噜，她就抓起一把锤子，直接走向爸爸妈妈的卧室。她踮着脚尖慢慢地走进去，小心翼翼地不发出一点儿声音，因为她不想让偷头发的贼听到。当她走到爸爸的床边时，她开始警觉地盯着她爸爸的头，决心等小偷一出现就抓住他。不一会儿，她看见她爸爸的头上有一个影子，于是她用尽全力把锤子砸下去。

嘭的一声！她爸爸大叫了一声，立刻从床上跳下来。他头上的包很大，

---

pilferer *n.* 小偷
snore *v.* 打鼾；打呼噜

snuffle *n.* 抽鼻子声；呼吸声
watchfully *adv.* 警惕地；警觉地

143

movement leapt out of bed. The lump on his head was already big, and growing. Trembling with shock, he turned the light on, and saw Valerie *brandishing* her hammer in the air.

"I nearly got him, Daddy! I thought I hit him, but it looks like he escaped!"

Meanwhile, all the commotion had woken Valerie's mother up. Seeing the lump on her husband's head, she burst out laughing.

"Well, that's what happens when you tell silly stories," she said, highly amused.

So Valerie's father had to explain to her that the hair thief didn't exist, and that going bald is something that just happens naturally to most daddies. There he sat, with a huge lump on his head, realising just how important it is not to tell children tall tales. And Valerie still worried about her daddy, but she no longer lay in wait for the hair thief. Instead, she bought her daddy a very nice sleeping *bonnet*.

而且越来越大。他吓得直发抖，把灯打开，看见瓦莱丽挥舞着锤子。

"我差点就抓住他了，爸爸！我想我打中他了，他好像逃跑了！"

同时，瓦莱丽的妈妈也被吵醒了。看见她丈夫头上的包，她忍不住大笑起来。

"这就是你讲荒诞故事的下场，"她笑着说道。

瓦莱丽的爸爸不得不向她解释，根本没有偷头发的贼，大多数爸爸的头发都会越来越少，这是很正常的。他坐在那里，头上顶着个大包，意识到不要给孩子们讲荒诞故事是多么的重要。瓦莱丽还是很担心她的爸爸，但是她再也不会不睡觉等着偷头发的贼出现了，而是给她的爸爸买了一顶非常漂亮的睡帽。

---

brandish *v.* 激动地挥舞   bonnet *n.* （带子系于下巴的）童帽；旧式女帽

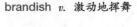